MINIMALIST

10 Steps to Declutter, Organize, and Simplify Your Life You Wish You Already Knew

Table of Contents

MINIMALIST

Introduction

1 Evaluate Your Priorities   1

2 Evaluate Your Belongings   4

3 Look At Where Your Time Goes   10

5 Establish A Clutter Free Area   15

6 Learn To Travel Lightly   20

7 Go Through Your Clothes   23

8 Look At Your Goals   28

9 Cut Down On Screen Time   33

10 Create Limits   41

11 Live Purposefully   47

Conclusion

MINIMALIST LIVING

Introduction

1 What Is Minimalism: Minimalism Vs. Materialism   58

2 How Can Minimalism Improve Your Quality Of Life?   64

3 Step- By- Step Guide To Becoming A Minimalist   69

4 10 Tips To Living Like A Minimalist   74

5 Take Five Minutes   78

6 Decluttering Tactics For Any Room In Your Home   84

7 Creating Space In The Bedroom And Kitchen   91

8 Minimalistic Techniques For Improving Your Health   97

9 Money And Minimalism   102

10 Simplifying The Internet And Technology   107

11 Getting The Most Out Of Your Personal Relationships   112

Chapter 12   The Modern Minimalist Movement   117

Conclusion   121

MINDFULNESS

Introduction

1 Where Did It All Begin?   124

2 What Is Mindful Based Stress Reduction?   129

3 The Basic Tools Toward Mbsr   132

4 Further Methods For Specific Situations   137

5 What Mindfulness Does   143

Conclusion

Introduction

So what is minimalism? It is very simple: to be considered as a minimalist you have to live with no more than 100 items. You cannot own a car. You cannot own a home. You must not have a career. You will live in countries that you can't pronounce. You have to have a blog. You won't be able to have children. The most important rule is you must be a white male, who's young and who comes from a privileged background.

Yes, obviously joking. Minimalism is merely a tool that can help you to find freedom. Freedom from depression, guilt, being constantly overwhelmed, worry, and fear. Freedom from feeling trapped by the consumer culture that we have built our lives around. We are talking absolute real freedom.

There's nothing wrong with owning things. Problems we have seems to be the underlying reasons why we need stuff. We have the tendency to give meanings to our stuff. A lot of times we forget to take care of ourselves. We forget about our personal growth, passions, relationships, and the desire to help anyone or anything but ourselves. Do you want a house or car? Wonderful, go for it! Dream of having a career and family?

If this is important to you, that's wonderful. Minimalism just allows you to be about the be more conscious and deliberate about these decisions.

Minimalism can help you:

- Discover purpose in your life
- Rid yourself of too much stuff
- Contribute to others
- Grow as an individual
- Focus on your health
- Consume less, create more
- Experience real freedom
- Discover your true mission
- Pursue your passion
- Live in each moment
- Reclaim your time
- Get rid of your discontent

By putting minimalism in our lives, we will finally be able to find true happiness, and that is what everyone is looking for. Everyone wants to be happy. Minimalists search for happiness but not through things, but by living life. So, it is up to you to decide what is necessary for your life and what is in excess.

A quick warning: it will not be easy to take that first step. Your journey to minimalism will get much easier, and a lot more rewarding, the farther you go. The first steps will make radical changes to the way you think, your habits, and actions.

Don't worry about it; this will help you through the process. By the time you get to the end of the book being a minimalist will be second nature to you.

1

Evaluate Your Priorities

When you start becoming a minimalist, you have to do a complete analysis of your life. This is the most important step in simplifying your life. This step must not be ignored. What you need to do during this assessment is to find out what is most important and valuable to you. Figure out what parts of your life add the most value, meaning, and happiness to your life. By doing this, you will help to set your priorities right. It will be much easier to start the process when you have a clear understanding of what is important to you. By prioritizing, it will help you start to understand why minimalizing will benefit you by make sure that there's ample space for the essential things in your life. If you don't have this understanding, you won't feel comfortable in getting rid of things that aren't important to you. If you want to stop watching television, you could have a hard time if you don't know why you don't want to watch television. If you realize why you want to stop watching television is so that you can have more time with your family, you will be able to see the reasons behind it. Start assessing your life by writing a short list. Write down what is important to you and concentrate on these first. Focus on making room in your life for all your priorities gradually.

Make a list of the reasons why you want to live simpler. If you are tired of debt collectors, just write it down. Upset that you don't have time for your children? Write it down. Can't sleep at night because you are too stressed? Put it all on paper. Would love to fire your boss? You need to write that down, too. These are all the reasons why and these will give you leverage when you start to think it is just too hard to go forward. These "why"s will help you to remember what matters most.

These steps might be able to help you evaluate your life and get your priorities in order:

• Make a list of everything that is important to you. Your nightmares, dreams, goals?

• Prioritize this list in the order of importance.

• Do your friends support you or do they get you into trouble?

• Do you let others define you or do you make your own identity?

• Do you approach love rationally and calmly or do you get too caught up in emotions?

• Do you still have your inner child or has age made you cynical?

• Do you envy others' success or are you happy being the best you that you can be?

• Do you realize when you have made a mistake and can handle it or does it shadow you forever?

- Do you feel like your job traps you? Are you in a panic because you don't have a job? Is your career going as you had hoped?

- Are you active or do you need to make an effort to get into shape?

- Can you face the reality of life, the unexpected successes, and the missteps or are you stuck in the past and denial?

- Do you like your family or is the relationship strained?

- Do you let setbacks ruin you or can you pick yourself up and get on with your life?

- When you think about you, what do you think about? Are you happy with you?

2

Evaluate Your Belongings

Once you have gotten your priorities set, now it's time to think about your possessions. Think about everything you have and figure out if these align with what your priorities. Leave nothing unturned and question everything. See if what you own add value to your life. Or do they just distract you and cause noise. It 's hard to admit it, but your possessions might just show that you have too many things that have no value. These might be entertaining or fancy belongings, but deep down we know that they really don't add any real meaning or purpose. They just waste our time, empty our bank accounts, or drain our energy. Make a list of everything you own that you no longer value. You will need to start slow and just get rid of a few these belongings each week.

Throw away anything that you have two of. Take a walk through your house with a container and put all your duplicates in it. If you have two sets of storage bowl, put one in the container. Do you have more than one copy of a CD or DVD? Put it in the container. Whatever you have doubles of, put it in the container. When you have filled the container, put a label on it that says duplicates. Put it out of your sight for one month. If you haven't needed anything in the container or can't remember what is in the container, get it out of your house by donating it to a charity of your choice.

So when does clutter become a problem? For some clutter could be an energy zapper. Clutter can cause them to waste valuable time looking for things that can't be found. In very extreme cases, people might suffer from depression or obesity when their life of consumption goes beyond just things. When clutter turns into hoarding, the house gets so full that is has created fire hazards or other health problems if dust and mold are present. These extreme cases are very rare.

Here is a guide to help you declutter your home. It has been broken down into three parts to make it slightly easier. The first part gives you tools to help you be successful at getting rid of clutter. Part two walks you through the tips for each room. The third section helps you keep the clutter out of your house forever. With these instructions, clutter will not have a place to hide anywhere in your house.

How to Declutter

1.   Set Goals

Make a plan before you start. It doesn't matter how much clutter or how many rooms you have, if you set goals it will reduce your frustrations as you go. Keep these tips in mind:

- Write down all the spaces you want to tackle.

- Grade each space on severity.

- Do one space at a time.

- Set a completion date for each space.

- Plan extra time for areas where it is going to take longer.

2.   Make a Sorting System

You need to set up a sorting system for the items you find. You can make your own or use the ever popular three-box method. This method causes you to make a decision with every single item. This way you won't end up with a huge mess that you don't want to clean.

Find three containers and label them as keep, get rid of it, and storage.

For the keep container, you need to empty after you have completed a space. These items need to be put into their designated place.

Get rid of it container also needs to be emptied after you have finished a space. Store the items you are giving away or want to sell outside the house. Put them in the attic or garage temporarily. Write yourself a note and put it where it can be seen, so you don't forget about these things.

The storage container needs to be emptied as well. As you fill the container up, label it or place an inventory sheet inside so you will know what's inside the container.

There are several different ideas about what you can do with the get rid of its box. You could recycle, donate, have a garage sale, or rent a dumpster. It does take some time, but recycling paper, plastics, and glass helps our environment. Household item, shoes, and clothing that are in good condition can be taken to your favorite charity. You could make a little bundle of money back off all the items you find that you no longer need or want. If you find that you have too much stuff to get rid of that can't be recycled or donated, you can get a dumpster for the items that you just want to throw away.

3.   Be Willing to Get Rid of Junk

If you have clutter, you have junk you can throw out. It might not be junk, but it is not useful any longer. Getting rid of old things is the hardest part of decluttering. Some items you find will stir up memories and have a high sentimental value. These are valid feelings that will make it hard to get rid of.

You have many options when it comes to doing away with clutter, so you won't feel guilty about putting things in the trash. You must prepare both your mind and body before you start decluttering. Keep the following in mind if you find yourself struggling to get rid of an item.

The 80/20 rule usually refers to clothes. We normally only wear about 20 percent of the items in our closet 80 percent of the time. This rule holds true for toys, DVDs, books, video games, and more. The mission is to do away with what you don't use 80 percent of the time.

Don't think about what the item originally cost, see if it can add value to your life now and in the future. Understanding this concept will help you make rational decisions about what you should toss and what to keep.

If it doesn't work, throw it out. If you haven't used it in the past six months, get rid of it. If you don't absolutely love the item, get rid of it. Once you have made a decision to get rid of the clutter, sleep on it. If you can't live without it, you will know it in the morning. Pull it out and put it away.

1. Work on Flat Surfaces

Flat surfaces like shelves and counter tops are magnets for clutter. Small appliance, magazines, bills, and mail will take over the flat surfaces in your home. Is this the place to put them? No.

Keeping a few things on your counters is fine but make a rule to keep your flat surfaces clutter free.

2. Keep Similar Things Together

Keeping similar things together will force you to keep your home organized. It makes your life easier, too. Store these items where you use them, and you will know where they are if you need them, but it reduces the small frustrations in your life.

Now that you have the essential tools for decluttering use them and declutter every room.

3

Look at Where Your Time Goes

When becoming a minimalist isn't just about decluttering with physical objects but by getting rid of time-wasting activities as well. You need to figure out how you spend your time. Ask yourself if what you do adds value to your life. By doing this will help you spend less time doing unproductive and time wasting activities. This will give you freedom for the activities you enjoy doing. Look at every activity and everything you do. Write down the time you spend on less necessary activities. See if there are things the bring no value to your life. See if what you are committed to is in line with your priorities. When you have an understanding of how you spend your time, see if you can get rid of activities that are not beneficial to you. Start slowly by working on the most pressing problems, one by one. You could get rid of just one bad habit instead of fighting with a lot and getting nowhere.

The people that you spend time with have a big influence on your life. It is logical that you want to have relationships with encouraging and positive people. Minimalism is finding out who the toxic people are in your life. Figure out who drains your energy and does nothing but waste your time. Spend less time with the ones who discourage you from chasing your dreams.

Most people understand this simple fact: time is the most non-renewable resource in the universe; you can never get it back. However, hardly anybody tries to analyze the way that they spend their time every week. Even fewer don't keep track of what they say are important to them with how much time they will actually spend doing this.

Try to sort everything that you must do and everything you are responsible for into categories. These, of course, will be different depending on the person and what they do.

Improvement and growth will focus on opportunities and not on crises. The challenge is not to let the less important needs crowd out the important ones.

Most people agree that speaking and communicating with others is absolutely essential, and they're right to think so: people are social animals. Everything we know is based on what we've gathered from and built upon with others. However, few people set aside any time to communicate. In the everyday hustle and bustle, communication inevitably suffers as people scramble to do necessary chores that range from assessing resources all the way down to responding to e-mails. After you have seen the numbers of how much time people spend doing these sorts of things, you will be in shock.

Ask yourself what you want to accomplish and what would be the best way to use what time that you have. To come up with a real and worthwhile answer to this question, you need to factor all the competing claims for your time like cooking, cleaning, driving children to and from school, household errands, spending time with friends, grabbing a coffee, helping with homework, whatever it may be. When you have assigned percentages, you need to figure out the actual hours for each category. Does your day have enough hours in it to do everything you need to do? To actually be useful, you may need to change up what you do monthly, weekly, or daily.

Since you have figured out how to leverage your time, you just need to be fierce in executing it.

You must audit your time. Take out your calendar and see if you have met your time allocations for each of your categories. This will let you know if you need to adjust anything going forward. Keep track of how you spend your time.

Auditing your time will show the patterns of your distractive tendencies, and show you how and when you absolutely lose sight of the things which are truly important. Does multitasking work for you? Some people experience a writer's block, so to speak, when they are juggling more than one task at a time, or moving from one task to another. Generally, the more difficult of a task that you are trying to move to, the greater the time and energy expenditure will be. This means that it will take a while for you to pick up the task in question, acclimate yourself to it mentally, and fully get into the groove of things. This process is only exacerbated by more difficult tasks. These time and energy costs could reduce your efficiency by about 20 percent.

Some people benefit greatly from to-do lists. However, in general, to-do lists are only useful to people if they are to set the specific amounts of time that they want to spend on each task while creating the list. This notion of time management, of course, doesn't come easily to most people. To work on and perfect this concept, whenever you make a to-do list, you need to estimate just how long each task will take to complete, and do your best to meet that timeline. If you don't meet that timeline, then you know to adjust your time-budgeting for that activity in the future. If you find yourself working on a new sort of task and aren't sure how much time to estimate for it, absolutely ask people who have done it before.

Bear in mind that if you ask someone else to do what you can't or don't like to do, these weak points will come back to haunt you. Instead of putting the work off onto others, you should instead recognize where you aren't as strong as you'd like to be and learn how to build yourself up from there. Most people only manage their lives through crises. They only set priorities between problems. To be effective, you must focus on opportunities and change your schedules as you need to. If you don't have something that is more important come along, you must discipline yourself to do everything as you have planned.

Don't try to multitask. A lot of people pride themselves on being great multitaskers. Some say that multitasking doesn't really exist. It is just a fairy tale or myth. Don't fool yourself into thinking that you can. Just by believing in something will not make it true. Research shows that the brain does not have the capability of multitasking. In reality, all you are doing is going from one activity to another. This decreases your productivity drastically. You shouldn't try to clutter your life or workflow with trying to do too many things at one time. Focus on just one thing. Do what you need to do with great attention and care. Get rid of any distractions and ignore the temptation to multitask. Concentrating on and completing one task at a time will make you more productive. It will increase your concentration and have an impact on your work. Minimalism is all about focusing on what is important with your undivided attention.

5

Establish a Clutter Free Area

You need to create a zone that will always be free of clutter. It could be the kitchen table, a nightstand, a section of countertop, or just a drawer in the kitchen. Use that zone as an inspiration to start living with less. If you start to enjoy that clear, clean environment, then expand that zone just a little bit more every day. A countertop that's free of clutter could soon become a room that's free of clutter. A room free of clutter could become the minimalist home that you have been dreaming about.

As we've talked about before, flat surfaces will attract clutter faster than any other place. All that stuff that's piled on these surfaces makes it impossible to use those surfaces. You have to move things around so that you can cook or eat a meal or just be able to put your feet up and relax. It's almost impossible to find anything, and it looks horrible.

But, we just keep piling stuff on top of stuff on top of stuff. It's just easier than putting things away where they go. To have success in keeping your flat surfaces clear, you have to find places to put your belongings. If you are fed up with cleaning off your surfaces just to have them disappear again and again under piles of junk, these strategies could help.

Create a non-flat place for everything that you bring home. The human's natural reaction is to drop everything that you have in your hands on the closest surface, as soon as you walk through the door. Start paying attention the next time you walk in your door. What are you holding? A purse, phone, keys, mail, coat, possibly grocery bags? Figure out where you need to put these items. Hooks are easier to use than hangers. If a chair back is the target for your coat, hang a hook.

If smaller items are the problem, think about hanging some totes or baskets on additional hooks. They are easier to clean out so you can change the contents when you need to. These should be large enough to hold everything from dry cleaning, projects, and books.

Keep kitchen utensils and tools off your counters. Kitchen counters get cluttered very easily. If your kitchen is limited on workspace, this becomes a big problem when you try to cook. A way you can take the clutter off of your counters is by using wall hooks to hang your cooking tools. Floating shelves, magnetic rails with S-hooks, or pegboards could all be used to store knives, spices, and utensils. They will still be within reach but out of your way at the same time. If you enter your home through the kitchen, put up some wall hooks and baskets to hold your mail, keys, etc.

Keep your counter space for your everyday necessities. Those small appliances don't really feel small when they take up all your counter space. Limit it to just the small appliances you use every single day. Store everything else in cabinets.

So the appliances aren't too hard to put away when done with them, make sure they aren't too heavy. You could put the other small appliances on a cart and roll it out of the way when they aren't needed. Wheel in the cart to use what you need to and put it away again.

Keep your dining room table set at all times. A set table has a very clear purpose. You will be less tempted to clutter it up. Every evening when dinner is finished, clean the table off and set out the breakfast things. This will help encourage a clutter-free table. It will also make a smoother morning routine. When breakfast is over, set out the placemats and dishes for dinner. Your table won't be as tempting to throw your things on when you get home. If you have kitties who are curious and like to walk on the table when you aren't home, you could set some candles, flowers, or even a stack of dishes with a cloth across them to protect them from curious paws.

Watch out for multipurpose spaces. Spaces that share two different purposes such as a dining room and home office might just be the hardest to keep clean. Having specific, obvious, and easy storage is what makes a space function well. The storage should be clear and simple so that anyone can put their things away. Having wall-mounted files with labels are a great option for your home office. If your craft space shares a room with something else, get a cabinet with doors and fill it with clear containers to easily see your items.

You could try a tilted desk. If you can't keep all those paper piles off of your desk, a desk that tilts could break that piling habit. You won't be able to have a desktop computer. If you want to stop the piles from just migrating to another spot, get a paper organizing system that is easy to maintain. You could try some stacking trays or just some shallow drawers.

Make a bin for old clothes. The flat surfaces of the bedroom like chairs, dresser tops, floors, and the bed become a catch-all for the clothing that just gets worn once but might get worn again before laundering. Instead of dumping these items on the closest surface, make a home for them. Use an open-top bin or a basket since putting it in a basket is just as easy as throwing it on a chair. If you have a closet system, clean out a drawer or basket to use for this. You could just have another laundry basket to use for this.

Make your bedside table neater. Do you need your sleep? Of course, you do. We all do. You need to make a restful environment around your bed. Having a cluttered nightstand won't achieve this. Don't try to make room for every single this you think you need on your nightstand. If you like to read, have one book. If you write in a journal, have the journal and your favorite pen there. You could have a glass of water and pretty it up with a candle. That's all you need.

Avoid having catchalls. Having a basket or tray on your counter or coffee table to catch clutter does seem like a good idea. It is until it starts flowing all over the surface around it. Clutter will attract more clutter. When random little items like pens, buttons, loose change, or hair ties all get put in one spot, you will probably start adding larger items like dry cleaning, shopping bags, or mail to it. You need to make a spot for every type of item. Have a jar for coins. Use fun cups or small buckets for pens. Hang hooks for keys. Place baskets for mail. Get a drawer organizer with small sections for little items like stamps and hair ties. Putting things in their respected containers will be satisfying.

We have talked about clutter attracting clutter. You might think it's not a big deal to set that bag, brush, envelope on the table. The problems it that someone sees that one item and puts another one with it. It continues until it becomes a dumping ground for clutter.

It isn't easy making a no-clutter zone, but it is very effective. Clean everything off of, let's say, the coffee table. Try vigilantly to protect it from getting cluttered again. You will find it easier to focus on one goal instead of many. If you can stick to decluttering one surface at a time, it will soon become second nature to you.

6

Learn to Travel Lightly

The next time you are getting ready for your vacation, try packing the minimalist way. Pack for just half of the time you will be gone. If you are going for four days, just pack for two. If you need to, you could wash something out and hang it up to dry. You could wear the same thing again if you had to. You will be surprised at how it feels to carry less luggage.

Let's look at packing a suitcase for a minimalist.

The first thing you have to do is reduce. I can't say it enough. Reduce. Even if you don't have that many clothes already, you probably still have a few things you haven't worn much that you could throw away. You might consider making a maybe stack and a definite stack. Take a look at the maybe stack and ask these questions:

1. Do I like the way it fits?

2. Is it easily cleaned? Does it need to be dry cleaned?

3. Can I wear it for just one occasion or many?

4. Is it suitable for different types of weather?

5. Does it go with anything else I own?

6. Have I worn this in the past six months?

These are apparently targeted toward clothing, but you could do the same thing with gadgets or toiletries by asking:

7. Do I use this a lot?

8. Can I get a replacement quickly?

9. Could I get this where I'm going?

10. If I don't take this, what's the worst thing that could happen?

By systematically looking at every item and going through some things in your head sounds like it could take forever, but it only takes a few minutes to decide if something is worth taking.

Sort everything out. Decide what goes in your suitcase, and you are taking as carry-on. You also need to decide what you will be wearing on the flight. If it is weather fit, wear your bulkiest stuff, that way you can put more stuff in the suitcase.

When you have finally decided on what you are taking, it is time to begin packing. Folding and putting the clothes on top of each other only works for dresser drawers and everyday clothing. You can't do this in a suitcase. There are other ways to pack your clothes and save space as well.

One solution is that you can roll your clothing into cylinders, there is another method where you lay out all the clothing flat in a different direction and fold them around a center core that can be anything from a makeup case to smaller clothing that won't work well for the outer layers.

The pile was originally 32 cm folded the regular way. When folded the other way it shrank down to only 20 cm. This saves about one-third of your space. The bundles are a whole lot easier to handle as well.

Arrange your suitcase. Once you have the clothes bundled, now it's time to pack it all in the suitcase. You may have to do some Tetris maneuvers, but you should be able to fit everything in your suitcase. A few quick tips for the women out there to be able to pack your things just a bit tighter. Use the insides of shoes and the space created by heels to pack underwear and socks.

Zip it shut, and you are ready to go or wait. It will depend on when you or your flight will leave.

7

Go Through Your Clothes

If you haven't ever thought of Project 333, which is dressing with 33 items for three months. This includes accessories, jewelry, shoes, and clothing. Sound extreme? Maybe, thousands of people have tried it and loved it. They say it actually makes life a lot easier instead of being more challenging.

You've heard the saying that clothes make the man. You probably haven't heard that clothes make women go crazy. I'm here to tell you why they do.

The best way to say it is that fashionistas are just a bit obsessed. You could say this might go in the crazy good category. Then you have to I don't care what I look like dressers. Then there are the ones the care, but they struggle finding what looks right for their body type. That means these people usually just wear the same articles of clothing over and over again. You might like to shop for inspiration. You buy things you liked in the store, you bring them home, stuff them in your closet. Then the first time you pull something out to wear it, you don't like the way it looks on you. So it goes back into the closet where it stays for eternity. When friends come over and look in your closet, they are met with a closet full of clothes. But yet, here you are in the same baggy t-shirt and jeans you always wear. Winter sees you in jeans and sweaters.

The main problem here is that your closet keeps getting bigger and bigger because you have an unhealthy obsession with shopping without truly knowing what you are looking for. So, why can't you find what you really want?

Let's say you haven't gotten rid of any clothes since you were in your 20s. You are closing in on 40, so the clothes you wore in your 20s just aren't appropriate anymore. Then there are the clothes you wore in your 30s but you've gotten married and had children since then, and those just don't fit the way they should. So you find yourself at a clothing crossroads. It can be painful.

There are days when you walk into your closet, and you get that nagging voice telling you that nothing is going to look good. You're going to look horrible. I wouldn't dare try that one again. By the time you get halfway through you just automatically reach for those jeans and a t-shirt. You walk out a bit depressed and sad. Wishing above all that you have something you could put on to inspire and excite you.

That's the point, though, isn't it? You want clothes that you won't question. You don't want to be out and about and have that panicky feeling that you want to go home and get in your feel-good clothes. So, why risk it? All those clothes are hanging in your closet just

24

hanging around waiting. You don't want to tell yourself negative things but how can you not when you walk into your closet and can't find anything that inspires you. You might be a new mom and have worked hard to get your body back into shape. You just need to find a calm fashion sense but how do you do it?

So here is the closet diet. You need to do the most dreaded thing ever – get rid of everything you don't wear. All of those articles that you might wear or I will fit into it again have to go. Make a few different piles. Make a pile for your favorite charity. Make one for the clothes you want to resell. Have a garage sale and make some extra money or take them to a consignment shop if you don't have the time to have a garage sell. By doing it this way, you know where all your beloved clothes are going.

Do a little bit at a time. Cleaning out a whole closet can take some time. Don't rush it. If you have children, it might take a bit longer. Nap times are the perfect time to tackle this mission.

Start color coordinating. This alone can be a life changer. The rainbow is fantastic because it is visually pleasing. Grab something neutral, and then you can add a pop of color to mix it up.

Put all your clothing into categories. Simply this means pants go with pants, shirts with shirts, etc. By using this approach, you will be able to find the garment you want. You won't be standing there looking for a blouse staring at the skirts.

Make the cuts just a tad but deeper. Don't be afraid, be brave. Get your clothes down to a Zen pallet of clothes that you will actually wear. That means getting rid of any wild prints that aren't in style anymore or those neon colors we all loved back in the day.

You will have an identity crisis and possibly get depressed. Your closet will be clean but what happened to all the "fun" clothes? Where are your wild prints? Then you panic and think you don't have enough clothes. You've thrown out too many. You have nothing to wear. Where did you put your crazy fun side? You have turned yourself into a boring old mom. This isn't me!

Just wait, and something wonderful will happen. You will notice there isn't a bunch of chaos playing through your mind as you start to the closet. You will feel different. The inner voice was usually mean. Now you are looking forward to not being overwhelmed by your clothes. You realize that the closet diet is actually working.

You can apply this to shopping as well. Instead of buying whatever to fill a hole, you know what you will wear, and you start to buy clothes thoughtfully. You can add some flair but don't overdo it with insane prints or vintage pieces. It is okay to admire them just don't put them in your closet. Grab a few floral prints or sequined tops.

You will find yourself months later happy, and your closet life will finally be sane. You won't be doing battle each time you get dressed. You will know what works for you and you can learn to be kind to yourself. Yes, your body has changed after becoming a mom. It is your responsibility to set an example for your children. We must empower them and send them good messages. We can't tear ourselves apart and expect these behaviors to go unseen by our children. Just remember it is about what makes you feel good and what works for you. Just like your closet, you have to make space for better and bigger things. It will never hurt to be wearing a cute outfit when you do it. It will be one that came out of your nice new closet.

8

Look At Your Goals

I'm sure you have goals. We all do. This is what gets us up every morning to pursue our dreams. Our ambitions and goals will significantly shape our lives that we live. Not all our goals are beneficial. Not all our goals will fit into a minimalistic lifestyle. It is extremely important to look at and see if your goals are still working with the priorities that you have set. Ask yourself if pursuing these goals will, in fact, add value to your life. Take time out to reflect on the outcome your goals will bring. Will it be worthy of your effort and time? You will also need to reduce the number of targets that you pursue. Don't waste time on many goals that you pursue half-heartedly. Instead, focus on setting just a few goals and pursue these with diligence and attention. You can get radical by just minimalizing to having only one goal. It will help you reduce stress and concentrate on your highest priority goals.

In the past, when you've tried to prepare and plan specific goals, you have most likely also set maybe-specific, maybe-not timelines by which you'd like to see the end result manifest.

You probably never thought that you would need to review your goals because you might be able to feel or see the goals that you've set working before your very eyes.

But this raises the question: what do you if you don't see them? What should you do if your deadline pops up, yet the goal that you set for yourself that hasn't been achieved?

You need to review and evaluate your goals and do this regularly, maybe once a week.

So what do you do if you don't see results? You might start feeling no motivation or get to the point where you just say, "Why bother? I can't see results."

If you are taking action and are 100 percent committed, then right now is a great time to actually take a step back and look at how your goals are going.

You just might not be able to realize the exact results you'd like to in a matter of moments.

You might get discouraged on not being able to see. Most of us want to see that concrete evidence that everything we are doing is actually going to wind up being worth the effort, but unfortunately, things normally don't really work out that way.

Why do you need to evaluate and review? You might notice little results. You might not have seen as much of a result as you would like to. This is why you need to tweak your goals just a bit to get to the outcome. You might figure out that changing the way you are approaching just one little aspect of your goal might just explode your results.

Evaluation is needed because it and keeps you honest about the efforts. It might show you the logical gaps in the plans that you're established, and it may also give you the energy and ambition to keep going even when there aren't any obvious results happening for you.

You should evaluate periodically two different ways. The first one is assessing your daily actions.

You should never leave your goals hanging. Staying committed when you can't see any results is critical. It may just seem easier just to forget them, but this is the point at which you really should try to have an honest one-on-one with yourself. Better yet, look for somebody you trust that you can honestly and candidly speak to, but somebody who is also on your side. They might offer you another perspective or might be able to give you some new ideas.

You can't just leave them hanging just because it is getting a little hard. You are just wasting time. You may be only one step away from reaching your goal.

Every couple of weeks, take some time to answer these question honestly:

1. Are you staying with your plan?

2. Can you improve your plan?

3. Have you moved on to your plan B?

4. Did plan B work for you?

5. Can you improve on your first plan?

6. Does anything need to be modified?

7. Did these modifications work for you?

8. Did your results meet your expectations?

9. If they didn't, why didn't they?

10. Is there anything you can do to get better results? Meaning go back to your original set of how, when, where, why, and who question – is there anything that you could feasibly add to your protocol or program so that you can see better results?

This other set of questions should be answered on a monthly basis. The focus of these questions is to focus on the long-term results of our efforts rather than the banalities of day-to-day program regimen:

1. Is everything that you're working on going where you'd like for it to go?

2. Do you have the same goal, or have you thought about a

change?

3. Are there ways of improving the plans and the regimen that you set initially?

4. Throughout the process, have you learned anything about yourself as a person?

5. Throughout the process, have you learned to appreciate various parts of yourself more?

6. What habits and qualities still need to be improved upon?

7. How can you start expanding your potential and stretching your limits?

8. Have you thought of larger goals you want to achieve?

9

Cut Down on Screen Time

All the time we spend with electronic gadgets brings a lot of unnecessary noise into our lives. Plus, the mindless consumption of media will actually add more problems instead of fix them. If you spend the majority of your life consuming all the different forms of media like newspapers, the internet, movies, and of course television, all of these will shape how you feel and think. The longer you spend with all this media; the more authority it will have over your life. Your actions and thoughts will be overtaken by media if you allow it to control your life. It will affect how you look at life and have an effect on what you believe in. The biggest problem is trying to understand the influence that media has on your mind. This was difficult to do if media are affecting the way you think. There is only one way to find out the bad ways media is affecting your life. That is by removing them from your life. It is easy to just shrug it off as craziness as long as media has its influence over you. It will amaze you the huge difference that turning off and disconnecting your electronics can have.

If you have started to declutter your house, you know how much more fresh energy it has brought into your home. Just like having an uncluttered computer will make a more productive, fresh, and enjoyable experience. Never underestimate its value. These benefits will outweigh the amount of time that it takes.

To keep digital consumption at a minimum, work on these areas to declutter:

Work on your inbox messages. You take the mail out of your mailbox every day. So, why can't you apply this same principle for your email? If you can reply to an email in under two minutes, do it immediately. If it is going to take longer, place it in a folder for later.

What about your old documents? Do you absolutely need everything that is in the documents folder? I doubt it. You could actually delete most of them and never think about them again. If you don't want to get rid of them entirely, move them to archives, so they aren't cluttering up the most-used folders.

What to do with old apps, programs, and software? Uninstalling something is entirely different than just deleting it from shortcuts. By uninstalling a program will free up space on your hard drive. Deleting the shortcut doesn't do this.

Get rid of some of those desktop icons. Remove the images that you do not frequently use. This is the same thing as decluttering your desk. Having a clean workspace allows you to concentrate better on the tasks at hand.

Have a good folder structure. If you don't mind spending a whole lot of time looking for a document in a particular folder, then you can skip this step. If this bothers you, then read on. To get started, you need to rename all folders that have the name of a new folder. Delete all folders that don't have anything saved in them. Develop a structure that will work for all who use the computer and files.

Photos are the hardest to get rid of. You have to get rid of any photographs that don't have any purpose. You don't print up horrible photos and put them on display. So, you don't need to hang on to them and let them continue to take up hard drive space. By hanging onto these bad photos makes it more difficult when you want to find a certain one when you need it. Delete them as you are going through and editing them.

What about your movies and music? The most beautiful thing about digital media is you have all your movies and songs at your fingertips when you want them. Unfortunately, the worst thing about digital media is having every movie and song at your fingertips. So they won't clutter up the library, delete the ones you don't use immediately. If you just can't bring yourself to delete them, simply move them to another folder where you can find them if you need them. I'll bet that you won't need to.

Watch how much time you spend online. You need to log on less. Your children will be thanking you. Spend that extra time with your kids. Get back outside and enjoy the sun. Instead of taking your tablet to the park, bring a Frisbee or your child's favorite outdoor toy, and don't forget the dog. Have a great time but above all enjoy your family.

Watch out for the number of friends you have on Facebook. If you have too many friends, it will make it harder to stay in touch with the ones that you really care about. Seeing that a friend from high school is taking her children out to eat is interesting, but all that never-ending newsfeed keeps you distracted from the ones sitting near you. Yes, it is fun to join in and see just how many friends you can get, but you have to realize that you are no longer in high school.

Watch out for the time-wasters on Facebook, too. Keep track on how many groups you join. Cut down on the number of games you play. Poke fewer people. Turn your chat off now and then.

Moving on to Twitter. You don't have to spend your entire day on Twitter to get anything out of it. Twitter is just like a river. You can get in it and feel the water. You can bathe in it. You can even frolic in it. You can jump out at any time. You can get back in it whenever you want. You don't need to try to navigate the whole river. That is impossible and a big waste of time. Here are a few tips that you might find useful:

1. Don't follow too many people.

2. Don't start tweeting all the time.

3. Don't stay on twitter all day.

4. Make an announcement.

5. Ask questions.

6. Find a conversation and add to it.

7. Reduce the number of inboxes.

Look at your RSS subscriptions. Get rid of any blog subscriptions that haven't been updated in a while or that are not relevant to you anymore.

Check your internet bookmarks. Delete all the bookmarks that you don't need. It is very simple to do just right-click and delete. For the markers that you still need, just put them in a folder to find them quicker.

Don't forget about your cookies. If you don't know what a cookie is, it is just a little packet of text that gets saved by the web browser to store information that is unique to you and your internet history. These are considered harmless, but a significant percent of advertising comes from the information that your computer gets from tracking cookies.

Get rid of your old contact information. Easy as it sounds. Delete the contacts that are no longer needed. Update your contact information that needs to be updated. This keeps your folders efficient and clutter-free.

Keep track of your log-ins and passwords. It can get hectic if you have many sites that you log into. You have the option of writing them down and remembering where you put your paper, or you can check out some websites like 1Password.

Watch out for email marketing. There is nothing I hate more than to open my email and it's nothing but ads. Unsubscribe to advertisements and newsletters that are no longer relevant to you. You can't just delete the message. Scroll to the bottom and click on the unsubscribe link. It only takes a few seconds to go through their requirements to get you unsubscribed.

How many email accounts do you have? Nobody needs any more than two. One for work and one for personal. If you could just have just one, it would be great.

Look at your desktop background. Learn to appreciate the beauty of a simple background. The background shouldn't be cluttered. It shouldn't clutter your mind or eyes. This improves your productivity and helps with attention span more than you realize.

Find your temporary internet files. Click on your control panel. Now choose internet options. Click on general. Then delete temporary internet files. Simple as that you are done.

Change your internet home page. How many times have you logged on and get bombarded with celebrity gossip, sports score, news, and politics? Every single day, I bet. One quick tip: Change your homepage to the un-personalized google.com. There are no headlines doing battle for your attention.

Defragment and disc clean-up. This usually only takes about four clicks on most computers. Go to your start button. Find accessories. Now system tool. Finally, disc clean up. It usually takes some time to actually clean and defragment, but it is worth it.

Recycle your old digital devices. We all have old devices lying around like external hard drives, cell phones, MP3 players, thumb drives, and cameras. If you like making the most of your technology, you probably have a stash of old devices that you don't use. If you can't find someone that wants a used device, there are several websites that will buy back some of these. Check them out and see if you can put some money back into your pocket.

Watch out for that tangle of cables. You usually use your desktop computer on top of a desk. Duh. Do not allow this space to be overrun with things that beg for your attention and encroaches on your personal space like cables. Cables can be controlled with some zip ties and creativity.

Hardware manuals and CD-ROMS. If you no longer have a particular program on your computer, you don't need that setup CD that came with it or the manual for that matter. To reduce more paper clutter, you could see if your manual is available online. If they are, get rid of the paper one entirely.

There you have it. Yes, it is a rather long list, and it certainly can't be done in one day. It will take more time than you realize. And that's okay. Just do a little bit at a time until you get done.

10

Create Limits

When you are trying to become a minimalist, you will soon realize that there are activities or things that you just simply cannot or just don't want to get rid of. All of us have things that we do on a regular basis, and you just cannot do without them. You must have your phone, so you can make and receive business calls. You might need a computer and internet access to send and receive emails and to stay up to date on happenings. You might still like to read or listen to inspiring or funny podcasts. The key to all of this is the set limits. Don't let these take over your life. Don't allow them to interrupt your work. Focus on these activities during certain times. Set limits on how often you check your email. Checking them twice a day is plenty. Set limits for every activity you do. This will help you get and stay focused and be more productive.

Boundaries have to be set to have healthy relationships and life in general. Setting and keeping boundaries is a skill. Sadly, it's one that most of us don't learn. We could pick some pointers now and then from experience or by watching other. But most of us the boundary building is a new and challenging concept.

To have a healthy boundary means that you know and understand what your limits are.

Here are some ways to maintain healthy boundaries:

1. Name your limits. If you don't even know where you stand, you will not be able to set limits. Find out what your spiritual, mental, emotional, and physical limits are. Think about what you can tolerate and try to accept with will make you feel stressed or uncomfortable. These feelings will help you to identify your limits.

2. Tune into your feelings. Two key emotions are red flags that we are letting go of our boundaries, and they are resentment and discomfort. Think about these feelings as you would the pain level indicator from zero to ten. If you get to six, you are in the high zone.

If you are on the upper end of the indicator while you are interacting with someone or during a particular situation, ask yourself what is causing this? What is bothering you about this interaction or the other person's expectations?

Feelings of resentment come from either not being appreciated or being taken advantage of. It usually means you are pushing yourself beyond your limits either from guilt, or someone else's expectations. They might be imposing their values and views on you.

If somebody's actions make you feel uneasy or uncomfortable, that's a red flag that they might be crossing or violating a boundary.

3. Be direct. Keeping healthy boundaries with some people does not require a clear cup or direct dialogue. This happens when people have similar approaches to life, personalities, views, and communication styles. They usually approach each other the same way.

The ones who have different backgrounds or personalities, you will have to be more direct with your boundaries. One person thinks that challenging another's opinion is a good way to communicate. To someone else, it may feel like they are being disrespected and thus they feel tense.

You might also have to be direct in other situations. Time might be a boundary issue if you are in a romantic relationship. Partners will need to talk about the time they need keep their sense of self and how much time they want to spend together.

4. Give yourself permission. Self-doubt, guilt, and fear are potential pitfalls. We may fear another's response if we try to set or enforce our boundaries. We may feel guilty if we speak up or say no to another member of our family. Most believe that we have to be able to deal with a situation or just say yes since they are a healthy child, even when you feel drained or that they are taking advantage of you. You might even wonder

if you should even have boundaries at all.

Boundaries are a sign of self-respect. They are not just for a healthy relationship. Give yourself permission to set some boundaries and work hard to keep them.

5. Practice self-awareness. Boundaries are about sharpening your awareness about your feelings and then making sure you honor them. If you realize that you are slipping and not keeping your boundaries, ask yourself what changed? Think about these questions: What am I doing? What are they doing? What about this situation is making me feel stressed or resentful? Then check out your options: What can I do about it? What exactly do I have control over?

6. Think about your present and past. The way that you were raised and the role you played within your family structure could be an obstacle when it comes to preserving and setting boundaries. If you were a caretaker, you learned from a young age that you were supposed to focus on others. You were used to letting yourself get drained both physically and emotionally. Ignoring your needs were probably normal for you.

Think about the people that you are around now. Are the relationships complementary? Do you experience a healthy amount of give and take?

Look beyond your relationships. The environment around you might just be unhealthy, as well. If your schedule is usually for an eight-hour work day, but your coworkers stay longer, you have the feeling that you must stay that long as well. You have to do and be better than they are. It is very challenging when you are the only one who tries to maintain healthy boundaries. This is where you have to tune into your needs and feelings and honor them. This is crucial.

7. Self-care needs to be a priority. This involves giving yourself permission to put yourself in the number one spot. When you do this, your motivation and need to set those boundaries become stronger. Self-care means you recognize how important your feelings are and you honor them. Feelings give you important clues about your wellness and what makes you unhappy and happy.

By putting yourself first will give you the positive outlook, peace of mind, and energy to be there for others. When you are in the right place, you can be a wonderful friend, coworker, husband, wife, mother, father, or sibling.

8. Seek support. If placing and maintaining boundaries is a struggle for you, then ask for help. It can be a good friend, a coach, a counselor, a church member, or a support group. You can have family and friends help you to make keeping your boundaries a priority when you are together. You can hold each other accountable. You can find help through other

resources, as well.

9. Be assertive. You realize that setting boundaries is not enough. You have actually to follow through with them. You know that people aren't mind-readers, but you still think others should automatically know what bothers you. Since they have no way of knowing this, you must communicate well with others if they cross a boundary.

Respectfully, let them know exactly what bothered you and that you both can work through it together.

10. Start small. As with any new skill, learning to communicate your boundaries will take practice. Start with a small boundary that isn't that threatening to you. Slowly increase to more challenging one. Build each one upon the success of the others. Don't try to take on anything that you know will overwhelm you. Setting boundaries will take support, practice, and courage. Remember that this is a skill that you will master.

11

Live Purposefully

The last, but not the least, important part of being a minimalist is to learn how to live in the moment and do so with purpose. To be able to accomplish this is to switch your focus from the past and future to the now. Don't continue to think about how you could have done things differently or blaming yourself for something that is in the past. Also, don't sit and think about what is going to happen, you have no control over that. When you dwell on the past and future, you are robbing yourself of the power and joy of the present moment. Know that, unless you have a time machine, you can't change things that have happened nor can influence what will happen to you in the future. Instead, live now so that you can build the foundation of a great future. Also, use what you have learned from you past, mistakes or experiences, to shape your foundation. Living with purpose will give you more time to spend your life more valuably and with more meaning. Simplify things, and notice how it feels to live in the moment.

Saying that you should live in the moment is often easier said than done. You could also be thinking, "Well, how else do we live but in the moment?" Right, technically everybody's body lives in the moment, but their minds don't. After you switch your thinking from physical to mental, you start to see thing completely differently. You start paying attention to your thoughts you'll begin to notice that you are thinking about the past or future most of the time.

You may be thinking, "Then why isn't it called thinking in the moment?" That's a good question. It's not called thinking in the moment because you can feel, experience, a see the present moment, but you can't think about it. The human thought process is unable to think about the present moment.

When you start to think about things, your thoughts will become influenced by values, attitudes, mindsets, and past experiences. Your thoughts will always be influenced by something that has happened and not what is happening.

Your past and future are not able to be seen or touched, you're not able to physically experience it, and you can't feel what is happening in that moment. You are only able to imagine these realities in your mind.

The present is a thing that you can see, feel, and experience; which is wonderful because it is actual reality and not an imagined thought.

Instead of giving you explicit instructions on how to live in the moment, I'm going to give some reasoning as to why living in the moment is so powerful. There may even be some tips on how to start living your life in the moment.

Happiness and Gratitude

We're going to look at some psychology here. Maslow, in his hierarchy of needs, tells us that the motive that lives behind human actions is the needs that the person is looking to satisfy: self-actualization, social, security, physiological needs, as well as others. After you have fulfilled a need on one level, you automatically move to the next level of needs. Throughout our whole life, we are just trying to achieve the next thing that we need in a race for fulfillment.

This cycle will never end because you are in a constant race to feel happy, but once you accomplish one thing another pops up. When you live in the moment, you aren't making your happiness dependent on things you don't currently have.

Wealth is one of the main things that human beings try to accomplish, which will allow them to be able to buy things. The reasoning behind the need for money is hoping that they will be able to locate happiness and fulfillment by buying things. When you look at the people that do gain abundance in money, you will be able to see the shift in their hierarchy of needs after they discovered that money, wealth, and possessions aren't what fulfill them. Because of this, they start to try and reach the next level of needs.

With living in the moment, you learn how to be grateful for things that you have at that moment. It won't matter if it's health, wealth, or family. When you live in the moment, you aren't dependent on having gained wealth or other tangible objects to be happy; which will turn make you happy. You will also realize that the pursuit of material possessions with the hopes of gaining happiness will ultimately fail.

Being able to live in the moment is an essential part of happiness. You don't gain happiness by thinking about things, even if you were happy when something happened in the past. You are only able to experience true happiness by feeling it in your present moment. Happiness is never dependent on the wealth or stuff your own, but it does depend on your ability to be grateful for all the things that you do have in your life.

Worriless

There will be times in your life where you think you can't achieve something, or you won't be able to do something. You've probably already had moments like this. When you learn to live in the moment, you will no longer be plagued by these thoughts. You won't have thoughts of what will, could have, or might happen. You learn to accept things as they are and as they will be.

Rediscover Balance

Sit down and make a chart to see where you need the most help in your life. Make three sections: thrive, survive, and struggle. In each, write down which areas of your life you are thriving in, meaning doing well, surviving in, meaning you are doing okay and struggling, meaning you are barely staying afloat.

This will allow you to see what areas of your life you need to work on, and then you can set intentions to change them. You have to be very truthful with yourself when you do this. It won't do any good if you don't list the areas in the right space, not where you wish they would go. You're probably not thriving in everything at the moment.

Roadmap

To help you travel down the road of living life with purpose, here is a little roadmap to help along the way in case you get lost.

11. Incubate – sit quietly and look deep into you for your deepest intentions and desires. Take note of where this leads you

12. Notice – start paying attention to your actions and thoughts. Pay attention to what they let you know about the things that you find the most fulfilling and gives you the most sense of purpose. Then start looking for things that lead you to the truth

13. Trust – be confident in what your inner-self tells you, and what the universe tells you, and let that be your guide

14. Express – write all of your intentions down. Once you know them speak them out loud and let your friends and family know so that you can embrace them more fully

15. Nurture – you have to be gentle with yourself as you try to live in the moment. Your intentions won't be a simple and straightforward path, much like life itself, and allowing yourself to try something and fail is an extremely important part of this process

16. Take Action – after you have your intentions, don't sit back and hope it will come true on its own. Instead, you will have to take practical steps to make sure that your intentions can come to fruition. You may find it easier to set one intention and then set little goals that will help you achieve the intention.

Conclusion:

Again, thanks for downloading and reading this book.

I sincerely hope that this book was able to get you started on the road to minimalism. Remember, that this change isn't going to happen overnight. It is going to take time, but the more you hold yourself to make these changes, the more you will appreciate your effort.

The next thing for you to do is to start practicing these steps. The great thing about the previous 10 steps is that you don't have to do them in order. Do them in the order that seems to work best for you. Spend as much time as you have, especially on the decluttering one.

There is no need to rush into this headlong either. This is a race, not a sprint, so take it slow. You don't want to burn out on the first day, and then end up giving up. Good luck with your minimalist adventure.

Did you enjoy this book?

I want to thank you for purchasing and reading this book. I really hope you got a lot out of it.

Can I ask a quick favor though?

If you enjoyed this book I would really appreciate it if you could leave me a positive review on Amazon.

I love getting feedback from my customers and reviews on Amazon really do make a difference. I read all my reviews and would really appreciate your thoughts.

Thanks so much.

SIMON RUDDY

Minimalist Living

A Minimalist Guide to a Non-Materialistic Life

Introduction

I want to thank you and congratulate you for downloading the book, *Minimalist Living: A Minimalism Guide to a Non- Materialistic Life*!

Today, we are constantly under pressure to live up to the standards of living that materialistic companies establish for us. The way you dress, the phone you have, and the car you drive have come to serve as billboards for the rest of the world to know how much your job and you are worth. Every major holiday comes with a whole new line of commercials and advertisements that encourage you to buy the next great thing, or else you will be missing out on a great chance to show off what you can afford. Our worth is constantly challenged by corporations who benefit from the insecurity of always wanting more.

Minimalism is the answer to your desire to break away from expectations set up by a commercial- drive society. It is a way of life that allows you to let go of the fear of losing your money and possessions, so that you can enrich your life in other meaningful ways. In this book, you will learn what minimalism is, as well as the many ways you may benefit from this lifestyle. You will come to understand the negative effects that material possessions have inflicted on your quality of life, as well as how you can break away from the mindset of needing to fulfill your life with "stuff."

This book contains proven techniques and strategies on how to truly become a minimalist and live a simpler life that is improved through quality of experiences, rather than quantity of personal possessions. If you feel that you are ready to experience life on a whole new level, then it is time to learn and adopt the minimalist lifestyle. This book will teach out how to let go of your inherent materialistic behaviors and motivate you to be a more motivated and productive person in your day— to—day life.

It's time for you to find peace and happiness so that you can live a joyful life without the weight of money over your head. Minimalism will enable you to create deeper and meaningful bond with the people you love and allow your relationships to flourish without the expectations of money and objects becoming the foundation for successful connections. It is time for you to become free to live your life fully through simplifying your home and lifestyle.

Thanks again for downloading this book, I hope you enjoy it!

1

What is Minimalism: Minimalism vs. Materialism

Minimalism has become more prevalent than ever in our ever-growing materialistic society. With the commercial- driven mindset of large corporations and small businesses doing whatever they can do make a buck, it has become second nature to adopt a consumer mentality. We are always looking for the next great deal and ways to save money while still trying to fulfill our lives with new things. We look towards clothes, electronics, accessories, and smart devices to satisfy the persistent void of always wanting more. While millions of consumers have become fully indulged in this mental state, there is a community of commercialism rebels that is expanding. Minimalists are spreading the word about their unconventional lifestyle to bring awareness to the financial, economic, and mentally harmful effects of the materialist mentality.

So, what is minimalism? Most people tend to think of minimalism as giving up all of one's worldly possessions for a simpler life that is free from material distractions. However, minimalism is so much more than giving away all of your stuff. There are specific guidelines that help transitioning individuals to easily adapt to the lifestyle. To be a minimalist, you must live with less than one hundred things; this includes clothes, cars, smart devices, etc. Many people believe that to be a minimalist, you have to be privileged, start a blog, give up everything you hold dear, and a whole list of other ridiculous expectations. But, minimalism should be a personal choice that reflects your values and goals for pursuing the life of your dreams. Minimalism isn't about making the most of some sort of fad lifestyle and becoming lifestyle guru. If you have the desire to live with fewer material possessions so you have the opportunity to experience life in a new way, then minimalism is for you.

Minimalism is a gateway to helping you find freedom in life. Freedom from worry, stress, fear, guilt, and the culture of consumerism that feeds into all the feelings of entrapment within our lives. Minimalism will help you break free from the suffocated mindset of always wanting and needing more. By eliminating the amount of "stuff" you own, you are also cleansing yourself from future worries and responsibilities. With the newfound freedom, you can embrace life in an entirely new way; which will allow you to switch from a materialist to minimalist mindset so you can focus on the experiences you have, rather than the things you buy.

Becoming a minimalist does not mean condemning friends and family members who choose to live with the opposite lifestyle. There is nothing inherently wrong with having material possessions. We put so much meaning into material objects, which is why they have caused so much harm in our lives. Relationships, passion, self-development, and even health are often pushed aside or even reliant on what we own or what we buy for others. We are often judge based on what we own, can afford to buy, and what we give to others, as if our character is based off the amount of money we make rather than who we are. Minimalism allows you to enjoy life by appreciating what you *do* have, through making lifestyle decisions more consciously and deliberately than before.

Different Minimalist Lifestyles with the Same End Goals

The minimalist community is growing more and more each year. While the overall goal of minimalism is shared, there are still differences in each individual's lifestyle and personal goals. There are some minimalists who have kids, careers, and a simple suburban life, as well as young adventures who wander around the globe with just enough necessities to fit into a backpack. Although minimalism encourages you to give up all the extra things that you do not really need, it also enables you to pursue a purpose- driven life without being inhibited by material ties. But how can all these minimalists be so different in their lifestyles, yet still fall under the same category? This question confronts the original concept of what you believe minimalism is. Minimalist is a lifestyle of ridding yourself of overabundance in favor of pursuing what is more important in life— leading you to happiness, satisfaction, and freedom. So, while the community of minimalists may all lead different lives, they still pursue the same foundational concept. The basic goals of minimalism, regardless of your own desires and achievements, include:

- Overcoming discontent
- Creating and giving more while consuming less
- Following your passions
- Focusing on mental and physical health
- Restoring personal time
- Discovering your purpose
- Self-development and personal growth
- Living in the present moment
- Contributing to the community beyond your own personal world
- Living with true freedom
- Removing excess stuff from your life

Setting Yourself Up for Success

To establish any new habit, routine, and lifestyle change, it takes time to successfully seamlessly integrate it as part of your daily life. You need all of your willpower and motivation to overcome the challenges that not only come with creating a new lifestyle, but also the difficulties of giving up a materialist lifestyle. Minimalism is not an external challenge, but internal pursuit of happiness and contentment. This lifestyle helps people find freedom from external disarray, but each minimalist must also go the extra mile to find freedom and peace within their own hearts to truly become happy as a minimalist. To ensure that you set up a strong foundation through this transition, here are the key elements of a successful minimalist lifestyle.

Living with Intention

Minimalism is not something that you just decide to do one day and hope that it all works out in your favor. It is a change of behavior marked by purpose and intention that must be felt every day. Minimalism is the intentional decision to remove the things that distract us from truly valuing the things that matter most in life. If forces you to reevaluate what your own personal values and goals are, so that each act moves you one step closer towards achieving your dreams.

Freedom from Possessions

The new age culture of consumerism has made us believe that the value of our life can only be reflected through the things we own. Modern lifestyles have fed us the lie that the more we own, the richer and better our lives are. But the happiness of buying and consuming is short- lived and minimal in the face of putting value in experiences and relationships over material things. Minimalism gives you freedom from the desire to possess. The minimalist lifestyle forces you to seek happiness in other areas of life, rather than material items. Through minimalism, you are able to blossom in all other aspects of life so you can truly enjoy living.

Freedom from Modern Chaos

Whether you live in a city or small town, there is no denying that there is a deep urge to get things done at a feverish pace. We are always rushing to do the next thing. We rush from the store to the doctor's office, then back home to make dinner, clean, put the kids to bed, etc. Life is a never- ending television drama, in which you feel your character just can't catch a break to breathe. Not only does this constant state of stress keep us from enjoying life, but our relationships, health, and mental state suffer. Minimalism forces you to slow down and frees your mind from being in the constant state of haste and movement. This allows you to live life with more intention and purpose, as you let go of things that have contributed to a stressful mindset. This simple acknowledgement alone will add more value to your life than any object ever could.

Although the transition from materialism to minimalism is difficult, the challenge is always resolved with a happier and healthier way of life. Minimalism is a lifestyle that can be achieved by anyone who wants to improve their life and create more meaning in their experiences. When you finally strip away all the material things in your house and closets, you realize how much time and money was spent wasted on things that you never really needed in the first place. You will come to value things that money can't buy: love, strong relationships, spiritual growth, a sense of purpose, and clarity.

Chapter 2

How Can Minimalism Improve Your Quality of

Life?

There are many life- changing benefits of adopting the minimalist lifestyle, aside from the general reasons to make the switch. From having more money to clearing more space up at home, there are several ways that you can benefit from choosing minimalism over materialism.

1. Focusing on Your Interests

There are many times when we sacrifice the things we love for the sake of making more money. This happens when we take a job offer that has nothing to do with our passion or when trying to earn overtime by cutting out quality time with your children. The sacrifices we make are usually reflective of good- hearted intentions. However, in the end, our passion and relationships tend to suffer. Minimalism is a tool that can clear your schedule, so you can enjoy the hobbies and interests that have previously been put off to the side. It allows you to stop spending time and money investing in shopping for things you don't need. The money and time you save can be put towards investing in your own passions and hobbies so you can actually enjoy doing the things you love and a much lower cost.

2. Less Focus on Material Objects

All of the "stuff" you have bought is just a distraction that you use to fill a sub- conscious void. Money cannot and will not buy you happiness. It can only provide temporary comfort. However, once we reach a level of comfort that satisfies our basic needs and desires, the obsession with material possessions and money should stop. We are constantly fed false promises from corporations that material possessions will bring joy to us and the people we love. But consumerism is a trap that feeds off your insecurities and desire to prove your worth through materialism. Minimalism allows you to let go of the desire to fill an emotional void with "things" and instead focus on building lasting fulfillment with experiences and relationships. Minimalism helps you realize that there is so much you don't need, and frees you from the consumer mindset.

3. Peace of Mind

We put so much value into the things we own that we are afraid of losing them. This fear of losing all of your possessions keeps you from becoming free of living without limits. Minimalism forces you to lose the attachment to these things, resulting a peaceful mind. You no longer have to worry about "what if's" and losing the stuff you have because it is no longer there, and you are no longer tied to it.

The less you have to stress about, the more peaceful your state of mind will be.

4. Fear of Failing

As parents, siblings, children, and friends we feel the expectations of our loved ones constantly. We are afraid that if we don't work enough, provide enough, and give enough, then the people we love will see us as failures. Regardless of your religious or spiritual affiliation, there is truth to the lifestyle that Buddhists lead in that they have no fear. This is because they have nothing to lose, and their gifts to others and to the world is their insight and presence. If you let go of the fear of losing all of your worldly possessions, then you can excel at any pursuit you take on. Minimalism faces you with the option of just living, without the fear of success or failure. You will finally enjoy life without expectations of yourself or others.

5. A Boost in Confidence

The minimalist lifestyle is a journey of self- reliance and individuality. Searching for a purpose and living out your mission makes you more confident as you learn the true meaning of happiness and fulfillment.

6. Spending Less Money

Now is your chance to really save money by spending less. As consumers who value money, we are constantly searching for the next best deal or greatest discount. Minimalism does not require you to buy more than what you need. By eliminating all the extra costs of purchasing material possessions, you can end up saving thousands of dollars.

7. A Cleaner Home

Cleaning is not a chore that many people look forward too; especially if your house is filled with useless junk that is scattered from room to room. When you are only buying what you need, instead of dozens of little things you simply want, there is much less clutter in your home. This makes it much easier to clean, even if you have kids who love to make messes.

8. Helping the Environment by Becoming More Sustainable

Landfills, waste, and pollution have seriously damaged the environment in ways that are almost unfixable. However, limiting the amount you consume does play a positive role in making the environment more sustainable once again. The less you buy and consume, the less waste there is that negatively affects the Earth.

9. Setting a Good Example for the People Who Look Up to You

Although the decision to become a minimalist is personal and rooted deeply in your own goals, you also prove to be a positive role model for the people around you. Your siblings, parents, and children will find valuable life lessons in your lifestyle that they will never learn anywhere else. The people who are inspired by your minimalist lifestyle will be more conscious of their choices and can fight against the materialist mindset.

10. A Chance to Make a Difference for Others

Everyone is recovering from the effects of an economy stuck in a downward spiral. Unfortunately, our own family's needs to save and pinch pennies has resulted in a lack of awareness to the needs of others who are less privileged. Money is only as valuable as the things you spend it on, which says a lot about your character and values. With the money saved from living a minimalist lifestyle, you can give back to the community, worthy causes, and families in need. And the gratitude you receive in return is much more fulfilling that material possessions.

11. You Will Appreciate Quality

You have heard the saying "quality over quantity" applied to many different areas of life: the friends you make, house you buy, etc. However, there is still a lack of appreciation for good craftsman ship that has caused corporations to mass produce cheaply made goods: which contributes to financial waste, as well as environmental waste. Minimalism allow you to form an appreciation for higher quality, as you invest your money into goods that last longer and are more sustainable.

3

Step- By- Step Guide to Becoming a Minimalist

So, you have officially decided to become a minimalist. Now, the question you may be asking is "where do I begin?" Minimalism is not hard to accomplish, but when you already have so much stuff, it can be difficult recognizing where to downside.

Step One

Start by asking yourself the following questions. The answers you give will begin putting perspective on the things you need, use, and truly value as opposed to items you don't really use but keep around anyway.

- What 3-5 things do you value the most in life? Does the amount of time you spend with these objects reflect the value you hold for them?
- Which part of the day do you most look forward to, and why?
- How does your living space affect your mood? Do you feel cramped, stressed, open, at ease, etc.?

- How many hours each day do you spend in a state of stress, worry, or anxiety? What are the surrounding circumstances that cause or contribute to these negative emotions?

- What is your favorite room or space in your home, and why?

- How often do you do the things you enjoy or do things just for the fun of it?

- What are some activities that always leave you feeling rejuvenated, happy, and energized?

- Which commitments that you have add real value to your day, and which do not?

- If you had one extra day each week to enjoy your time, how would you spend it?

Step Two

I.   Now that you have had time to reflect on what things add value to your life and which small ways will help to improve the quality of your life, it is time to begin separating your possessions into what you need, want, and don't need. As you sort through all of your belongings, it is easier to decide what items are more essential than others. Individuals who choose to adopt the minimalist lifestyle typically fall into three categories, depending on how willing they are to invest in a new way of life.

- I'm ready, let's get rid of everything.

- Not interested, I don't have a problem with buying stuff. I just need a bigger house.

\-   I'm interested, but don't know where to begin.

Start by separating your belongings into three separate categories:

1.   Trash, absolutely do not want or need, I can live without it.

2.   I think I can live without this but am not sure, I don't *want* to get rid of it, but it would be a shame to throw it out.

3.   I absolutely need this, I cannot live without this item, and there is no way I am getting rid of it.

II.   The next step is to write down your intentions with keeping some belongings and getting rid of others. Start by making a list of all the reasons you want to simplify your life, and how some tools or possessions may help you do so. Establishing your reasoning for becoming a minimalist will help put your efforts of separating what material possessions you want to keep, donate, or throw away. It will also assist you during moments of weakness, when getting rid of your things causes doubt in your mission of adopting minimalism.

Step Three

Make a space in your home that is always clutter- free; whether it is the kitchen table, a desk, or spare room. This mess- free area can be used for inspiration to live with less and serve as a reminder to live simply. When we are surrounded by mess and clutter, our lives seem more chaotic; which makes it difficult to be productive and function with a clear mindset to serve our purpose. You can start small, and then work your way to clearing out your entire house. Begin by clearing out a small space in one room, and gradually work towards cleaning and minimizing the entire room. Do this with every room in your house until you have created an entire clutter- free zone and you have completely transitioned from materialism to minimalism.

Step Four

The minimalist lifestyle is not just about creating a simplified state of your home, but in downsizing every aspect of life. One of the most expensive weekly and monthly bills is food and groceries. Between eating out, shopping at the store, and buying a morning coffee, food bills really add up at the end of each month. You could save hundreds, if not thousands of dollars each year by following the minimalist lifestyle. Obviously, saving money when buying food is not always simple. Bills vary each time you go to the store, especially if you have children who love to snack. However, you can still save and practice minimalism by eating the same thing for lunch or dinner at least two times a week and rotating your meal choices throughout the week.

Step Five

Always, always save whenever you have the chance! Minimalism can open many opportunities, if you know how to take advantage of the lifestyle. One of the key benefits of minimalism is saving money. Now that you have decided to live with less and do more with your money, you need to be consciously aware of how you decide to invest your money. You should always have an emergency savings account in case something should happen that would require immediate financial relief. In addition, you should immediately pay off any debt that you might have. This is the first step towards financial freedom. The second step is saving additional funds to invest in doing the things you love: traveling, treating your friends, taking your family on vacation, etc.

4

10 Tips to Living like a Minimalist

1.   Start clearing space in your home in short "waves" rather than all at once. Decluttering your home all at once can become overwhelming, and minimalism is supposed to clear stress from your life, not cause it. It can even prove to be more impactful if you slowly declutter our home, as you won't feel pressure to minimize quickly when you may not have the time to spare. However, once you have repeated this process several times, it becomes more difficult with each effort to simplify your home.

2.   Find your motivation with minimalism by establishing deadlines for your goals. It is easy to become distracted by everyday chaos; like work, taking care of your kids, exercising, etc. Getting swept up by day-to- day activities can keep you from accomplishing your goals and achieving a true minimalist lifestyle. Write down your goals, keep a journal, place post- it notes around your house, and keep a dream board in your bedroom. Keep yourself motivated and working towards living the life of your dreams.

3.   Look for new ways to give back to the world. As a minimalist, you recognize that there is not much you really want or need. You can use your new lifestyle to give back to the world by helping people and communities in need. Donate the things you've cleaned out of your

house and the money you save each month to make your mark on the world.

4.   Look towards a support system to help you make this life-changing transition. Making any lifestyle change can be very difficult, even for someone who embraces change. Confide in your friends and family about this new challenge in your life and ask them for help as you look for ways to achieve your goals. If you want your family to also make this transition with you, you must realize that you may not be able to convince them, as some people are simply not as open to change as others. But, you can still lead by example and do your best to be a role model for the people you love.

5.   If you are having a hard time getting rid of some personal items, consider investing in temporary storage. Some items carry more importance and meaning than others. Having to choose over so many things that you love and want can really make minimalism difficult. If you find yourself hung up on objects that are hard to let go of, place your things in a storage space so you can sort them later when you have decided whether or not you want to keep them. This will help your transition as well as easily clean out your home of things you don't use or need.

6.   Do not let yourself become distracted from your goals. Minimalism comes with intention, which is easily mistaken for action. Many times, we become too focused with the intention to make a change without actually taking action to make it happen. Remind yourself to act on your goals every day so no time is wasted in achieving your dreams. The benefits of minimalism can only be experienced once

you have full transitioned into the lifestyle; which can only happen by making a conscious effort every day to be a minimalist. Even just one small step each day will make a world of difference.

7.   Keep less than thirty- three items in it. While you do need clothes, there really is no other reason for having to many when you become a minimalist. However, you still want to make sure that you are fitting you style and dressing needs for every occasion when you make the decision to get rid of items from your closet. By limiting the amount of clothing you have, not only are you freeing up space, but also making your morning routine more efficient. As you empty your closet, you will come to realize just how much clothing you own that you actually wear. This will make getting rid of extra that much easier.

8.   Minimalism is not just about space and material possessions, it is about your state of mind. A psychological form of materialism is the modern dependency for smart phones, computers, and televisions. While technology has improved our lives in many ways, it has also contributed to over-active mental states. Our brains become so stimulated by our screens, that relaxing and breaking away from technology has become increasingly difficult. Therefore, you should take time each day to consciously put away your devices and enjoy alternative activities. In just a few days, you will realize how much stress and energy went into keeping up with all the social media notifications, emails, television shows, and other distractions.

9.   Invest in experiences rather than material objects. It has become more common for people to sit on their devices and dream about doing things, than actually going out into the world and experiencing life

themselves. Use the time and money you save from becoming a minimalist to invest into creating new experiences and looking for new and exciting ways to live your life. The memories you make will be much more significant than a collection of useless stuff.

10.   Remember that any lifestyle change takes time. You will have to work every day for months, even years to achieve a complete state of minimalism. You will have to resist the temptation to buy more stuff and spend money almost daily. Regardless of whatever difficulties you might face, you will achieve your goals and become a minimalist. Don't stress about how long it will take, or how many times you may splurge on an impulsive buy. Stay motivated, continue working towards your goals, and never give up!

Chapter 5

Take Five Minutes

Now that you have a working understanding what minimalism is and how it can benefit your life, we will now look at some concrete ways that you can work towards living a more intentional life through the space that you have in your home. When you're first turning your attention towards minimalism, it's important that you start small. Regardless of the room in your house that you're trying to declutter or the amount of stuff that you have, taking baby steps towards your larger goal is important so that you don't become overwhelmed or frustrated. To reach a minimalist end, it is not necessary to completely overhaul your entire life in a matter of weeks or even months. By repeating small actions on a frequent basis, you'll likely be able to live your life more fully because you will have less stuff cluttering your home base.

People who are just beginning to turn their attention towards minimalism will often take just five minutes per day and devote it to this new way of life. Of course, you want to make sure that you're spending these five minutes with intention and with precise actions that will help you to achieve your greater goals. Spending five minutes of your time working towards achieving minimalism in your home will help you to develop better habits and will also help prevent a situation where you're burnt out and give up on your goals.

Create a Decluttered Region in Your Home

The first five minute tactic that you might consider implementing is one where you pledge to keep one small space in your home clear and decluttered, no matter what. A great way to accomplish this activity is to start with a small amount of counter space and decide that you're going to keep this area completely de-cluttered no matter what. Try this for a week or two, taking five minutes at the end of the day to make sure that this area is as clean as possible. If you're relentless and committed to this task, there is eventually going to come a day where you find that this area of your home is always clean. After you've reached this goal, the next step is to broaden your decluttered region to encompass a larger space. This may mean broadening the counter space that you're committed to keeping clean, or it may mean even keep two counters decluttered all of the time. For this five-minute tactic, the idea is that you're gradually widening your decluttered zone over time, until one day you'll look around and realize that your entire home has become one giant decluttered region.

Plan Your Decluttering Weekend Ahead of Time

No, this five-minute task does not mean that you take five minutes to declutter your entire home in a single weekend; instead, this five-minute task is one where you check your calendar to see when you'll be able to schedule a decluttering weekend for yourself. This five-minute activity will help you to prioritize your minimalistic pursuit and make it easier to plan ahead instead of trying to fit minimalism into your already-busy life. Once you've taken the time to schedule this weekend, do your best to make sure that you don't cancel it or put it on the back-burner. When this decluttering weekend comes, take the time to relax, declutter, and work on creating more space in both your physical home and your mind. The other tactics presented in this book will help you to figure out how exactly you want to declutter your home and your life, but scheduling a weekend for yourself is often the first step towards organizing your world more intentionally.

Take Everything out of a Drawer

If you have a "junk" drawer in your house, then this tactic might be of particular interest to you. Choose a drawer in your home or even your office that you know is not organized and then take everything out of it. Next, put everything that's in your drawer into three piles. These piles will be either trash, stuff that you're going to donate or put into storage, and stuff that's going to be put back into the drawer. As an aside, it might be a good idea to purchase drawer dividers prior to participating in this five-minute activity. Drawer dividers can help to create a more organized feel in a drawer, and can sometimes force you to be more organized without really paying attention to it. If you know that there are many drawers in your home that are cluttered and need an overhaul, try taking on a single drawer once a day.

Donate!

One five-minute activity that may make you feel good about the work that you're doing for yourself is to load up your car with donation goods. Often times, minimalists will set aside the stuff that they know that they want to donate, but then it will end up sitting in their home, waiting to be brought out to the car. While it's certainly a good thing that you've taken the time to figure out your unused stuff that is going to go to charity, the stuff that you set aside and leave in your house is doing nothing except continuing to clutter your home. After you've used one day to load everything into your car, you should spend the next day of your five-minutes researching where you're going to donate your stuff if you have not already done so. You may not currently know where you want your stuff to go, but often times once you do a little bit of research on the internet, you'll find that there are places to donate your stuff extremely close to where you live. If this is the case, the last step is to this five-minute activity is to spend one of your days actually going to the donation place and dropping off your stuff. This method is more like a three-day, five-minute activity. If you already know that you're someone who has the tendency to put this type of activity off, then breaking it up into three days might provide you with a better chance of success and follow-through.

Enjoy Your Progress

If you commit yourself to doing a five-minute minimalistic activity every single day, then you should also be sure that you're going to spend one day appreciating the work that you've done. There's really no point in doing all of the hard work that it takes to achieve a minimalist lifestyle if you're not going to sit back and enjoy it every once in a while. If you decide to make this one of your five-minute activities for a particular day, it's important that you don't spend this time unintentionally. Instead of letting your mind wander onto other topics, try to keep it focused on noticing the work that you've done around you and the progress that you've made. Doing this will help you to feel accomplished and hopefully motivated to keep going. It may even be a good idea to plan this as one of your five-minute activities every two-weeks or so.

This chapter should have been able to make you see how important it is to start slow when you're working towards have less clutter in your life. There are many other five minute activities that you can work towards that have not been identified in this book, but the tactics that were presented in this chapter are often the ones that new minimalists gravitate towards first. Everyone has five minutes. It's how you spend the five minutes that you have that matters.

If you're someone who has the tendency to "go, go, go", it's also important that you take five minutes at least one day and focus on recognizing the progress that you've made.

While minimalism is certainly about implementing activities and forming new habits, it's also about slowing down and being able to recognize the small pleasures that this type of living can offer your life.

Chapter 6

Decluttering Tactics for Any Room in Your Home

The previous chapter provided you with five-minute activities for you to perform so that you can slowly become acquainted with minimalism. This chapter can be interpreted as an extension of the last chapter in the sense that the general tactics in this chapter should be used after you've been doing the five-minute activities for a while. This chapter will focus on explaining methods of decluttering such as the trash bag method, the four-box method, the idea of the thirty-day list, and tips on how you can visualize what you want your home to look like and represent. While we will also look at how you can organize specific areas of your home such as the bedroom and the kitchen, the tactics presented in this chapter can be applied to any area in the house when you're ready to use them.

The Trash Bag Method

The name of this method is not exactly elegant, but the idea behind it is sure to make your home appear more effortless. This strategy may take you more than five-minutes per day, but when you're first starting out it will not likely take you more than fifteen. Choose an area of the home that is particularly filled with stuff that you know is trash, such as the garage or the basement. Next, fill up a large trash bag with trash and throw it away. Over time, it's going to become more difficult to throw stuff away because your clutter is going to diminish in quantity, until eventually you are only left with what you need. While it is easier to do this in an area of the home that is particularly more cluttered than others, you can use this tactic in literally any area of the home. If you commit to filling up one trash bag full of stuff in every room in your home, it's important to do your best to fill it. Make tough decisions as you're sorting through your stuff. Some questions that you can ask that will make throwing your stuff away easier include the following:

- Have I used this item within the last year?
- Do I have an immediate need for this item?
- Does this item hold real sentimental significance, or am I perhaps holding onto to an emotionally-triggered part of my past?

Again, when you begin using this method, it's important that you're decisive and only hold onto things that are of use to you *now*. Try your best to avoid the feelings of procrastination that may arise as you decide whether or not to keep a particular good. Lastly, remember that if the item in question does not hold much sentimental value, you can always purchase another one and replace the old one that you have.

The Four-Box Approach to Decluttering

Another strategy that you can use in addition to or in replacement of the trash bag method that was described above is what's known as the four box methodology. This method is often used and promoted by many aspiring minimalists. What you need to obtain before beginning this process is four boxes. Next, you're going to want to label each box with a Sharpie marker or you can print out big labels from your computer and tape these labels onto the boxes. Each box should receive one of the following words: Keep, Trash, Store, Donate. After you have these four boxes, choose an area of your home that you're going to target. Bring all four of these boxes into that particular room, and get to work. Go through your entire home and choose whether you're going to keep something, give it away, put it into storage for the time being, or give it to a charity. When you're going through this process, arguably the single most important thing to avoid is a situation where you're not deciding on what to do with the goods in question. If you're finding that you're avoiding these four boxes and are instead making a fifth pile for uncertainty, this is surely a mistake on your end. All of the goods in this particular room need to be analyzed for their importance and usefulness. If you avoid doing this for every item, then you are procrastinating on your minimalistic goals.

In addition to the mistake of creating a fifth pile of certainty, another mistake that people who are new to the four-box method sometimes make is that he or she will put too many of their items into the storage category. If you find that your storage pile is quite larger than your other three piles, then you will need to assess how you're going to go about being less lenient on yourself. As an aside, it's important to recognize a situation where you're not quite ready to partake in an exercise of this nature. If you're finding that it's extremely difficult to rationalize getting rid of your excess material goods, then you may want to take a step back from your outward minimalistic pursuits and instead look inward. Take the time to ask yourself why you're pursuing a minimalistic lifestyle and why it matters to you. Then, when you've found your answers, you can go back and try the exercises in this chapter and the previous chapter again.

Start a Month Shopping List

If you're someone who is prone to doing much of your shopping online, you're not alone. These days, it is often too convenient to avoid participating in online shopping. What's more, we are often also being constantly bombarded with emails that are endorsing sales on the stuff that we love on a daily basis. Instead of indulging your desire to partake in compulsive online shopping, you should instead consider creating a thirty-day list for yourself. This list does not have to be one that sits on the refrigerator. Instead, you can make it on an excel spreadsheet or even on your phone for convenience. When you find a good that you want to compulsively purchase with a simple click of your mouse, resist the urge to buy it right away. Step back and instead add if to your thirty-day shopping list. If you were to use an excel spreadsheet for your list, it would likely look something like the table that's presented below:

Thirty-Day List

Date of Initial Interest	Item in Question	Website Where Item is Found	Date of Decision
4/1/2017	Hat	Urbanoutfitters.com	5/1/2017
5/7/2017	Shelving Unit	Westelm.com	6/7/2017

As the example above shows, these are the types of items that you want to be adding to your thirty-day list. These are non-essential items that you may not necessarily need but would still enjoy possessing. The logic behind this strategy is that when you remove yourself from a situation where you feel as if you *need* to purchase something the moment you see it, you're able to truly think about whether or not you want to own it. I'm sure you have been in a situation where all of your friends seem to be purchasing a particular good, and you feel as if you need to buy it in the heat of the moment. The tactic of the thirty-day list seeks to reduce this type of purchasing habit. If after thirty days you come back to the list and still see a rational reason why you should own it, then you should move forward in obtaining it. On the other hand, if you go back to the good in question and don't see it's worth the same way that you did thirty days ago, then you can easily walk away from the item.

Visualizing Your Ideal Life

Go into a room and contemplate how you want the space to look, feel, and function. If you have trouble figuring this out initially, there are some questions that you can ask yourself to help your creativity along. These questions include some of the following:

-        What type of mood do I want the room to express when people walk into it?
-        Are there currently too many items on display? What important goods do I want people to see in this room?
-        Am I using my wall space efficiently? Could I be using more of my walls for functionality? Is there currently too many photos or paintings on the walls that clutter the eyes and the brain?

There are many additional questions that you can ask yourself regarding how you want the general feeling of a room to be, but we'll stay away from them to avoid getting too close to a discussion on interior design. If you're interested in learning more about minimalism and interior design aesthetics, there are countless websites that provide comprehensive detail on this topic.

Exchanging an Old Item for a New Item

This last concept is less of a tactic and more something to generally keep in mind. Even though you're a minimalist, it's safe to say that you're still going to be purchasing new goods now and again. Instead of accumulating more and more stuff over the long-term, you should consider getting rid of one item in a particularly category of your stuff and replacing it with something new each time you make a new purchase. For example, if you decide that you absolutely *love* a pair of sneakers, consider only purchasing them when you find yourself in a situation where you actually need a new pair of sneakers because your old ones are falling apart. When you look at your stuff through this type of lens, you are making your purchases more objective and functional rather than lofty and emotionally-based. This will not only save you time but also space.

7

Creating Space in the Bedroom and Kitchen

Now that we have looked at general decluttering strategies, it's time to get more specific. This chapter is going to focus on two of the most important areas of the home to keep clean, the bedroom and the kitchen. While these areas of the home are quite different in their overall functionality and how they complement the home as a whole, the decluttering tips for each of these rooms are similar in multiple ways. This chapter will look at both the unique aspects of keeping these rooms clean as well as the similarities that they share.

The Bedroom Closet

If you've ever been late to a business meeting or to go out with friends, you may have found yourself in a situation where you accidentally leave your room in a state that looks like it's been subject to a tornado aftermath. Clothes are strewn all over the place, jewelry and shoes line the walls with their debris, and everything is generally a complete mess. When you're looking to declutter the bedroom, you're most likely going to want to primarily pay attention to your closet first. The first step when addressing the closet is to make sure that the rest of your room is somewhat clean from the start. Next, you're going to want to take everything out of your closet, which is why it's so important that the rest of your bedroom is relatively neat and tidy. This step should be simple enough because it does not really involve much decision-making on your part.

Once *everything*, literally everything, has been removed from your closet, the next step is to determine what clothes you're going to keep and which clothes are being kept for unnecessary reasons. You will also want to go through your shoes, your jewelry and any other accessories that you currently own and determine whether you're going to keep it or give it away to charity. We talked about the four-box methodology of determining whether or not you want to keep what's in a particular area of your home, and that strategy can still apply here, but with a key difference. It's advised that you resist the urge to keep a lot of clothing in storage because you will likely never wear it. You will end up unnecessary amounts of storage space and cluttering your home instead of doing anything beneficial with these items. If you live in a place where the seasons change frequently, then having storage space for your clothing makes sense, but you should still seek to limit what you're storing, regardless of your home's climate. There are a few specific tips that will be useful for you when determining whether you're going to keep your clothing or discard it. These methods include Oprah's Hanger Experiment and the 12-12-12 Experiment.

The 12-12-12 Experiment

If you're finding that it's a bit difficult to determine what clothing you're going to keep and what clothing you're going to get rid of, the 12-12-12 experiment may help you to decide a bit faster. For this method, the goal is to choose twelve items in your closet that you're going to keep, twelve items that you're going to discard, and twelve items that you're going to donate to a good cause. It may sound absurd to only keep twelve articles of clothing that you're going to wear on a frequent basis, but there's no reason why you have to get rid of more than twenty-four article of clothing either to discard or donate at a time. If you're someone who owns a lot of clothing, you may want to do the 12-12-12 experiment multiple times over a longer period of time. The general thinking behind this method is the consideration of the fact that clothing's only purpose is to be worn. When we hoard our clothing, we are doing nothing except creating more laundry and clutter for ourselves. If we could avoid these types of nusances, why wouldn't we?

Oprah Winfrey's Hanger Experiment

Oprah's hanger experiment requires that you throw less articles of clothing away than does the 12-12-12 experiment, at least during the short term. First, arrange all of the hangers in your closet so that they're facing in the same direction. Then, as you wear your clothing, be sure that after you put it through the laundry and hang it back up that you place the hangers in the opposite direction than the other hangers that are all uniformly hanging in your closet. Over time, you're going to be able to tell which articles of clothing you wear on a frequent basis and those that are simply taking up space because the hangers of the clothing that you do wear will be facing in the opposite direction of the clothing that you don't wear. This will provide you with empirical evidence regarding what clothing you're wearing and what clothing is excess.

The 12-12-12 experiment and Oprah's Hanger experiment are uniquely different from anything that goes on in the kitchen because they specifically pertain to your clothing. Again, getting your clothing under control in your bedroom is something with which many people struggle, which is why this topic has been given its own section in this chapter. Next, we will discuss some tips that you can use to keep your kitchen clutter-free, and most of these tactics can apply to the kitchen as well as the bedroom.

Hanging Your Pots

One of the easiest ways to create more room in your kitchen cabinets is to simply purchase a wire hanging rack for your pots and hang them instead of store them. Of course, you're going to want to make sure that these pots are in somewhat good condition since they're going to be on public display, but another great aspect of minimalism is that when you are consuming less, you're able to enhance the quality of the goods that you own because you're spending less money on a lot of goods on a regular basis. Another tip that may prove to be benefical to you as you look to organize your pots more efficiently is to take an inventory of the pots that you currently own. Chances are, if you've moved in with a significant other or have acquired a lot of kitchen supplies over time, you're probably holding onto pots that you don't need because you have duplicates. When you take this inventory, be sure to match the pots with the lids that you have in stock. You should be looking to discard old pots that may still work but for which you have better replacements.

Along these same lines, it's become more popular to hang jewelry on nails or hooks instead of storing them in a jewelry box or in a drawer. If you opt to hang your jewelry in your closet, you won't even have to see the nails or hooks that are holding your accessories for you. In fact, the back of your closet is the perfect place for your jewelry to hang, along with perhaps a full-length mirror, a metal rod for your scarves, tall boots, or scarves, or even hooks where you can place your hair accessories. When you utilize creative storage areas such as the back of your closet door, you're able to open your room up to more minimalist ideals and values that were not possible before.

Organizing Your Kitchen Based on Frequency of Use

One last tactic that you can utilize in both the kitchen and the bedroom is to organize your goods based on the frequency in which you use them. This is arguably easier to do in the kitchen than in the bedroom because you will ideally by using everything that's in your bedroom on a frequent basis, but it is still a good tactic to use as you develop your minimalist habits. In the kitchen, you should be looking to store items that you use the least in the top cabinet shelves, while the items that you use on a daily basis should be placed on the shelves that are easier to reach. While we're on the subject, it's important to note here that holiday items like festive cookie cutters and decorative plates would be better kept in storage rather than comprise the contents of your kitchen shelves. Since you're likely only going to be using these items once a year, there's no reason why they should be conveniently stored.

While you certainly can organize your bedroom in the same way as you're going to organize the kitchen, you may come to find that you already largely organize your bedroom in this manner. The articles of clothing that you wear on a daily basis such as your under garments or socks are typically located in easy-to-reach drawers, and it's never too hard to give your articles of clothing their rightful "home". Of course, you may also come to find that this is an area of your bedroom that needs some work, in which case you should tweak your bedroom organization.

8

Minimalistic Techniques for Improving Your

Health

Of course, decluttering your home is important from a practical sense, but your health is paramount to any concerns that you may have about the organization of your home. This chapter is going to focus on how you can make your health tactics work for you, rather than the other way around. So often, health and exercise are topics that are seen as being activities that have a defined "right" way of operation. This is primarily how the minimalist philsophy differs from other types of strategies in regards to an individual's health. As a minimalist, you are aligning yourself with an ideology that does not view anything as being intrinsically "right" or "wrong". Instead, you are acting in informed and enlightened ways that are appropriate for your individual mind and body. This is the approach that minimalists take towards their overall health, and this can be seen through their approach to exercise in particular.

A Minimalist's Exercise Regime

A minimalist's exercise regime is relatively simple in the sense that he or she is going to only do an exercise activity that he or she finds enjoyable. What is the point in doing an activity if you can't find some pleasure in it? This means that if you've been an active cyclist for years of your life but have felt a bit burnt out lately, stop cycling and look for a new activity to enjoy for a while. If you're someone who is currently not doing much in the form of working out, find the courage and the energy to check out some different types of exercising activities. As with the other topics that have been discussed in this book so far, you can start small. There's no need to endure a challenging cross-fit class if you're not there yet. If you want to get to a point where you can endure such an intense workout, go for it; however, slowly work towards that. Go at your own pace and find enjoyment in your exercise activities on a daily basis.

The primary reason why a devout minimalist exercises is to relieve stress. To this end, it makes little sense to exercise for an entire hour or even forty-five minutes if it's going to cause you to feel exhausted or over-worked. As a minimalist who is interested in maintaining health in all facets of your life, you should be looking to only exercise for as long as your body feels comfortable. In order to figure out how long you should be exercising, you are going to likely have to test out some different time frames so that you can achieve the optimal exercise timeframe. Be patient with yourself, and work at full intensity only until you feel like you can't go on anymore. Work hard, but don't overdo it, and most importantly find a period of time for which you consistently exercise. You may find that this period of time is ten minutes, while a different minimalist will find that his or her preferred exercise time length is twenty-eight minutes. Every minimalist's exercise regime will be unique.

A Minimalist's Diet

From the minimalist point of view, food should not be used as a replacement for or a form of entertainment. Food is fuel. Even if exercising is not something that you're interested in doing at any point in the near future, eating for fuel instead of for pleasure is a great way to reorient your thought process. Americans in particular have rather unhealthy eating habits, with one big one being the tendency to snack while watching television. As a minimalist, you should be looking to do *everything* in which you partake with your full attention present. This being the case, constantly snacking while you're watching television is taking away from the attention that you should be spending on the television instead of your food. If you actually stopped to think about your hunger in these snacking moments, you would more than likely come to find that you're truly not even hungry. When you make decisions about eating based on the notion of true hunger, this is when you'll know that you're eating for fuel rather than for pleasure. This is an important step towards developing better eating habits for yourself. Additionally, it's widely known that eating well can compliment a lifestyle that does not include high-intensity workouts such as cross fit or endurance running. It's widely understood that diet is more important than exercise, and that as long as your diet is in check, you'll be able to do strenuous activities with more ease than would otherwise be possible. If you're young, you may not think that this matters, but things such as balance, bone density, and healthy joints will begin to matter as you age.

The Foods that A Minimalist Will Likely Consume

If you're thinking that a minimalist would try to simplify his or her diet, well...you would be correct. An ideal diet for a minimalist would be one that consists of no meat and very little processed foods. In the United States, it's widely understood that the meat is heavily processed and even treated with antibiotics. These are complexities that a minimalist would not want to deal with in his or her diet, because the contents of this type of food is generally unregulated and unknown to the common consumer. Additionally, processed foods such as anything fried is typically avoided by a minimalist, largely for the reason that these types of foods are unhealthy. A good rule of thumb to follow is to only eat foods that have easy-to-read labels on them. For example, if there are more than ten ingredients on a label and you don't know how to pronounce the words or know what they mean, then you should avoid them. The simpler, the better. If you do eat meat and are not prepared to stop, then you should at least look for meat in the super market that is labeled "free range" because this means that it was not raised in a farm where disease is more prevalent. Below you will find a list of foods towards which minimalists typically gravitate. If you're hesitant to try these foods, start by choosing a new one to purchase each week at your grocery store.

- Tofu
- Whole grains such as rice
- Quinoa
- Legumes
- Avocados
- All vegetables
- Fruits
- Nuts

9

Money and Minimalism

One of the most fundamental ideas surrounding minimalism and your job is thinking about whether or not the particular activity is worth your freedom. For someone who lives in a modern American society, this can sometimes be a topic that's hard to grasp for multiple reasons. Firstly, as soon as an individual enters the workforce, the biggest challenge that he or she faces is finding a proper career path for him or herself. Instead of taking the time to think about exactly what pursuit in life would make this individual happy, he or she is bombarded with the idea that making money is paramount to any type of personal pursuit. Additionally, the consumer-driven lifestyle that many people lead can contribute to a feeling that you can never have too much money. The American Dream can only grow larger with a better job or a nicer car, and it can sometimes seem like you're constantly climbing a ladder to reach an unnattainable end. These are the types of philosophies and ways of thinking that a minimalist is seeking to avoid, and going about how to aviod this can be accomplished in a number of different ways.

Should I Compromise My Freedom for This?

One of most important questions that you can ask yourself when you're thinking about your current career path or choosing a new line of work is "is this worth my freedom?" Your time is your freedom. You don't have to subscribe to partaking in the workforce if you don't want to, but many of us do out of a sense of obligation or duty. Of course, this is not to suggest that everyone should not be working in some way, what this means is that people often will partake in a working activity even though it may not necessarily suit their personal interests or long-term goals. While it can sometimes feel like our life is on a trajectory that has been predetermined, the reality is that we have the ability to choose whether or not we want to do something. Our choices do not have to be based solely from a financial perspective; however, if you have children or are taking care of loved ones it may be more difficult to view you career from this perspective, but you should still do your best to keep this in mind for the long term. No one wants to be on a career path where they feel miserable day-in and day-out, and yet for so many people this appears to be the trend. Make a commitment to yourself that you're going to resist the urge to fall into something simply for the money that's attached to it, and design your life in a way that is as personally fulfilling as possible.

This question of whether or not something is worth your freedom extends beyond your career. This question can apply to something as small as the new blouse that you're thinking about buying or the new car that you want with the expensive monthly payment attached to it. For each of these items, you should really be thinking about why this particular item is important to you. For example, if you want the new blouse because all of your other blouses are starting to look too worn or unprofessional, you could throw one of your older blouses away and replace it with the new one. This would be a practical reason why this blouse would be worth a portion of your paycheck or "your freedom". On the other hand, if you're thinking about purchasing a new car solely because your neighbor just got one or because you want people to know that you make a lot of money, you really should take some time to consider if these types of goals are ones that truly mean something to you. Doing anything for the sake of others will often not make anyone happy, and when you take the time to think about how the money spent on that car could instead be used to take trips or have other unique experiences, the illusion of the car's luxury may start to deteriorate.

Saving Money, Spending Less

When you align your lifestyle with everything that minimalism has to offer, you will likely spend less money naturally. You'll be thinking about consuming less, eating with more awareness, and shopping with more frugality. Your desire to be constantly buying material goods will likely go away, and you'll be left with only what you truly need. If you're someone who currently tends to live paycheck to paycheck, it's about time that you worked towards changing those habits. Once you've started to consume less, you'll be more open to figuring out what it is what you truly want out of life. You'll be able to save your money with those types of goals in mind, and this will likely provide you with a sense of accomplishment regarding the money that you're saving. If you're looking for a concrete tip on how to save money, you can start by working towards saving $1,000. A relatively easy way to accomplish this is to open up a savings account (if you don't already have one) and then put away a specific amount of money as soon as you receive your paycheck. The amount of money that you put away should be determined based on how much money you're currently making and how quickly you wish to grow your savings account. Another way that you can determine how much you're going to save is to think about how much money you want to have saved by a specific period in time. For example, if you know that you want to have you $1,000 saved in two years, you would have to put away roughly $42 every month.

Lastly, it's important to understand your worth as you move towards trying to spend less and save more. Many of us unknowingly define ourselves by the amount of money that we make or the types of material possessions that we have. These are the types of sentiments that minimalists are seeking to avoid, and it is entirely possible to define yourself through your experiences rather than through the goods that you own. By paying better attention to the people around you and recognizing the worth that can be found in your simple experiences on a daily basis, you'll find worth in the things that cannot be bought. This is something that many people struggle with, especially as the world becomes more technological, less personal, and more dominated by dollar signs than an authentic sense of being.

Chapter 10

Simplifying the Internet and Technology

These days, it's hard not to see the world as getting smaller and smaller. In large part, technology is the reason why this seems to be the case. All you have to do is log onto your favorite social media website, and you'll be immediately tapped into many different types of lifestyles in a matter of seconds. While it is hard to say that everything that the internet brings to the table is inefficient or useless, there are plenty of things on the internet that waste our time. In addition to sometimes being a time-waster, the internet also provides us with the opportunity to judge ourselves against others and this can serve to make us feel inadequate in a variety of ways. Social media sites such as Facebook, Instagram, and other types of sites that primarily uses pictures as a way for people to curate their lifestyles for others to see are typically the ones that can make individuals feel inadequate or like their life is less significant than someone else's. By developing your awareness of the tactics in the chapter, you'll be able to get a better grasp on the omnipresent nature of technology in our ever-evolving society.

Unplugging and Letting Go

Smartphone technology has led people to constantly have screens in front of their eyes, and these screens limit the ability that people to interact with their surroundings and their loved ones to the fullest extent possible. One of the first ways that a new minimalist can work towards cutting down on the amount of time that he or she spends checking email, texting, and playing on other types of applications that do nothing except waste time is to choose a single day of the week where he or she avoids their technology at all costs. Of course, some technology that cannot be avoided include the car or the computer if you work somewhere that requires your ability to use one, but you still have options if you do not want to completely remove technology from your life. For example, instead of completely unplugging you could instead choose to limit yourself to not going onto social media sites or personal entertainment sites for one day out of the week. Instead, you can spend this time participating in activities that are more personally fulfilling or gratifying for you, such as working on a house project or spending the evening with a friend instead of cooped up in front of your television. Doing this will likely relieve of you a feeling that you are constantly "going" all the time, and if you're someone who sometimes feels FOMO (fear of missing out), stepping back from your social media devices will also help you to let this feeling go, too.

Look Inward

Another tactic that you can use if you're feeling like technology is taking over your life is to simply choose to participate in a different activity every time you feel yourself moving towards opening your phone, watching television, or browsing the internet. What if instead of engaging in these types of activities, you instead looked to meditate for a small period of time or spent some time reading an engaging book? When you look inward and take the time to get to know yourself, you'll likely come to find that you're someone who could use a bit of R&R away from the hustle and bustle that technology brings with it. While it still is technically a form of technology, the application Headspace nonetheless can help you to works towards developing a meditation practice for yourself. This application guides you through a nightly 5-minute meditation practice. If you decide to use this application, it's likely that you'll forget that you were even meditating in the first place. Another tactic that you can use to step away from the hustle and bustle of the day ahead is to devote the first hour of your day to yourself. Use this first hour to collect your thoughts and get ready for the day ahead by avoiding the craziness that can often be found online.

Looking to Kindle and Other Types of E-Readers

So far, this chapter has looked at the negative aspects of the internet and how it can infringe upon a minimalist's life, but there are also positive aspects of technology for a minimalist in the sense that technology can be used to help declutter certain areas of our life. This can be particularly seen through the use of E-readers such as the Kindle. You're not alone if you feel like there's nothing better than the physical presence of a good book in your hand, but the reality is that if you're an avid reader then your collection of books is probably quite large. Rather than keeping an extensive library in your home, consider donating your books to your nearest library and going to visit them whenever you're in the need of an old read. You'll be giving your books to a good cause and at the same time you'll be making more space in your home for yourself.

Say Goodbye to Cable Television

If you currently subscribe to cable, you're likely paying at least $100 for the basic channels. This subscription might seem worthwhile if it wasn't for the fact that many of the shows on cable television are ones that have little to no plotline and are only capable of providing you with reality-driven drama. Minimalists value quality over quantity, and this applies to everything in a minimalist's life, including the television shows that he or she watches. Instead of subscribing to basic cable, you should instead consider purchasing a cable box or USB stick that allows you to download applications to it once it's been purchased. For example, the Apple TV costs around $150. Once purchased, you can then add subscriptions to free channels such as Comedy Central, A&E and the History Channel. You may have to purchase the hour-length or half-hour length shows that you want to watch on these channels, but they will run you around $2.99 per episode (and that's a high estimate). If you're looking to be even more frugal, investing in the Amazon Fire Stick is also a great option. This small USB stick plugs into the back of your television and only costs around $40.00. If you subscribe to an Amazon Prime Membership, you will be able to watch the shows that Amazon makes as well as free movies that are on their site for no additional cost. Regardless of the specific option that you choose, it's safe to say that you will be saving a lot of money when you decide that you no longer want to spend $100 per month on your television-watching desires.

Chapter 11

Getting the Most out of Your Personal

Relationships

While it would be nice to think that all of our relationships are consistently working in a healthy manner, it's unlikely that this is truly the case. As you have already seen from the other chapters in this book, the goal of a minimalist is to create space and efficiency in all areas of his or her life. Relationships are no exception to this rule. This chapter is going to look at what you can do to better your current relationships, and this includes developing an awareness for the types of people who you should allow to cultivate a presence in your life and those who you should try to keep out. This chapter will also look at some communication tactics that you can use with your family so that they don't become confused or frustrated by your decision to move towards living a more minimalistic life.

Recognizing Your Position in a Relationship

When you're looking to cultivate healthier and more meaningful relationships in your life, the first thing that you should do is look at your own actions and sentiment towards others. Similar to the areas of your life and your home that you want to declutter and clear away the excess, you are looking to do the same with the relationships that you have. When you analyze your relationships and your role in them, it's important that you try to look at them with as much objectivism as possible. If you are unable to do this, then you will not be able to give your relationships the due consideration that they deserve from a minimalist perspective. Objectively analyzing your relationships is not necessarily easy, and to help you along here is a list of questions that you can ask yourself regarding your relationships as you move forward:

1. What are my contributions to this relationship?

2. Is this contribution equal to the contributions of the other person, or do I give more?

3. Does this other person deserve more from me? Am I acting too selfishly?

After you've asked yourself these questions, the next step is to seek out the person who is at the other end of this relationship. Have a sit-down with him or her and let them know that you need to discuss the current dynamics of your interaction. When you do this, make sure that you know exactly how you're going to approach this person. It's a good idea to focus on yourself rather than focus on their actions first, because otherwise he or she may become under the impression that you've asked to talk to them so that you can attack their personality. After you've focused on yourself for a bit, you can then turn to how they're interacting with you makes you feel. You want to be very direct when you bring up how you want the dynamic of your relationship to change, because otherwise they could walk away from your conversation confused. At the end of this conversation, you should make it a point to let this person know how much you value their friendship or other type of relationship that you have with them. Let them know that if your relationship with them didn't matter to you, then you wouldn't be talking to them in the first place. Afterwards, take a step back and see how things progress. If you can see that this person is trying to work out a new dynamic with you, then you know that he or she is someone who you want to keep in your life for a long time. On the other hand, if this person backs away from you and does not try to foster a healthier relationship with you, then you know that it might be time to cut ties with this person.

No one wants to let a friend go, but sometimes it's the only course of action left to take. Often, we develop friendships due to proximity or because we have known the person for a long time, instead of cultivating a relationship based on common interest or growth capabilities. For example, if you went to college then this is a concept that might be familiar to you. Kids in college will often gravitate towards the other people who live in their dorm rooms, because these people are the ones with whom they interact on a daily basis. These room assignments are largely random, and just because you have developed a relationship with someone who lives in the dorm next to you, this does not mean that this person necessarily meshes with your innate personality traits. As a minimalist, you have a responsibility to keep your relationships as efficient as possible. If someone is straining your energy and your ability to live the most fulfilling life possible, then you need to consider letting go of this person in exchange for other relationships that are healthier.

Your Family and Minimalism

If you have children or live with someone who may not completely understand why you want to become a minimalist when you first begin, then you will need to find time to sit down and have a conversation with these people. It's not enough to simply start operating in a minimalist manner and expect the loved ones around you to understand why you're choosing to act in a different way. When you sit down to talk to these people, it's important that you express to them why it is that you're choosing to act in a more minimalistic way. You can talk to them about how the material possessions that you own are making you feel stressed, or hone in on the fact that constantly buying new things all of the time is not making you happy in the way that you once thought it would. By expressing exactly why you are deciding to change your ways through a discussion of the struggles that you are having with your old, non-minimalistic lifestyle, it's likely that your loved ones including your children will be able to have a better idea of why you're looking to change. Additionally, it's important for these people to understand that you're not frustrated or angry with them, and communicating these types of thoughts will also provide them with a sense of ease. While you can try to persuade your children or your loved ones to adopt a more minimalistic way of thinking, it is not required that you do so. Just as you are choosing to live your life in a more fulfilling way, you should also let your loved ones blaze their own trail. If they have questions about minimalism, certainly answer them, but don't push a new philosophy on them right away. Over time, you may be surprised to find that your children or your loved ones will gradually look to simplify their lives through the example that you're setting for them.

Chapter 12

The Modern Minimalist Movement

The minimalist movement began towards the middle of the twentieth century, but in recent years has come back to the forefront of philosophical thought, and this is in large part due to the fast-paced society in which we now live. This chapter is going to look at two of the front-runner's of the modern day minimalist movement, Ryan Nicodemus and Joshua Fields Millburn. These two men have taken the minimalist philosophy and have completely made it accessible for everyone who wishes to get more out of their life. By understanding how these two men think and the work that they're doing, you'll be able to gain more insight into the intracies of minimalism today. Additionally, the resources that these men have created for minimalists will allow you to continue your reserach on the topic of minimalism without having to search very far.

Ryan Nicodemus

Ryan Nicodemus began to see the minimalist movement more attractive after he already had a job in the corporate world and was making a six-figure salary per year. Although he had a lot of money, he found that he was always spending even more than he was earning. Debt plagued his life, and Ryan noticed that he wasn't happy even though he had money at his fingertips. This is the primary reason why Ryan decided to stop working in the corporate world and devote his life to simpler living. Today, Ryan only owns *nine* articles of clothing, and he spends most of his time as a lifestyle coach, promoting a minimalist way of living.

Joshua Fields Millburn

Joshua's mother died and he got a divorce all in the same year. These are the two major catalysts that pushed him towards living a simpler life. Millburn, while he also was making a six-figure salary in the corporate world, knew that his personal passion was writing and not managing retail stores (which is what he was doing in the corporate world). Millburn and Nicodemus were childhood friends who decided to ultimately team up and promote minimalism together. Today, they have been on Oprah and host a podcast and a blog called *The Minimalists*. On this website, you can find everything that you need to know about the topic of minimalism. These two have written about all assets of life and how to make them simpler.

Minimalism, Millenials, and the American Dream

A key reason why both Nicodemus and Millburn decided to cultivate a stake in the minimalist philosophy is that they understand the younger and evolving American generation. In this way, you can interpret Nicodemus and Millburn to be reacting to a phenomenon that is currently occuring. The millenial generation can best be defined as anyone who is between the ages of eighteen and thirty-five. These people entered the workforce just as the 2008 housing bubble popped, and for this reason they are often looking to save money wherever they can. Jobs were and still are somewhat sparse, and many of these college-educated people had to work jobs at which they were over-qualified, while still living with their parents because of the large amounts of debt that they had to pay off from their college loans. Due to these reasons, many millenials would rather spend their money on experiences rather than things, mostly because they don't have the money to spend on lavish goods. They're having to learn how to save their money, and in doing this they have become better at figuring out what they feel it is that they want to spend their money on. From this perspective, it is rather obvious that Nicodemus and Millburn are both reacting to a phenonmenon that was in front of them, instead of developing a philosophy completely from scratch. It can be argued that one of the reasons why the minimalist movement is so popular today is because of events like the 2008 housing crisis and the rise in student loan debt. Without these factors, Nicodemus and Millburn may not have such a strong foothold in the current climate of an average American's point of view.

Nicodemus and Millburn both see the American Dream as something that has in recent years deteriorated, and it is from this viewpoint that they look to create a new philosophy that is real and somewhat oppositional to the ideals of the past.

Conclusion

Thank you again for downloading this book!

I hope this book was able to help you to understand the minimalist lifestyle, and inspire you to make this incredible change in your life.

The next step is to use this guide to implement minimalism into your life. Minimalism is the most efficient way to simplify your life, find peace of mind, and save money. By using the tips and strategies in this book, you can achieve ultimate success and truly experience life in a new way.

Simon Ruddy's Minimalist Living

MINDFULNESS

A Life Changing Guide to Finding
Peace and Happiness in Your
Everyday Life

Introduction

I want to thank you and congratulate you for purchasing the book, *Mindfulness*.

This book contains proven steps and strategies on how to increase happiness and develop a deeper sense of inner peace, calm and self knowledge by learning to live in the moment rather than worry about past or future events.

Mindfulness takes old techniques that many religions have used for thousands of years and combines them with modern scientific study. Freed from myth, creed or hocus pocus we find ourselves left with a technique that is both simple to practice and beneficial to all areas of our day to day lives and general well being. These techniques can be combined with a person's own religious beliefs or used within the sectarian context.

Thanks again for purchasing this book, I hope you enjoy it!

Chapter 1

Where Did It All Begin?

Most of us live in a world permeated by technology, unprecedented means of communication, rapid transport facilities and household appliances designed to make our lives easier. One would suppose that the primary benefit of all of this wizardry would be that we would be able to slow down a little, take our foot off the gas pedal and just cruise for a bit. Nothing seems to be further from the truth. Somehow society seems to have developed a momentum all of its own and many people feel that the pace of their lives are now out of control. Liker hamsters on a wheel we seem to move faster and faster without making any noticeable advances. Sure, we have more material goods but what good is all this 'stuff' if we are too stressed or tired to enjoy it.

Research shows that this deep sense that we have somehow missed the point of life and are instead heading in a direction not of our own choosing is now very widespread. Take a moment to have an in depth conversation with any of your close friends, colleagues or family and you will suddenly learn that this almost unidentifiable feeling of disquiet has become almost universal. It often leads to a sense of helplessness, frustration and dissatisfaction that, in extreme cases can damage both our relationships and our health.

The aim of this book is to offer a scientifically tested and approved pathway back to deeper inner peace and a greater awareness of what is causing our simmering, but hard to pinpoint, loss of equilibrium. The exercises you will learn here are not difficult or based on some form of self trickery. They do, however, require you to be patient and self forgiving. The rewards, often starting after just a few weeks, will be a greater sense of inner balance and peace that can have spillover effects on your health, relationships and even the way you eat. They do not require you to go and sit in an ashram on some isolated mountaintop or to spend untold hours in a difficult to achieve yoga stance. All you do need to do is to gain a better understanding of how your mind works and dedicate a few minutes each day to de-stressing and improving your mental state.

Many of us think nothing of spending hours each week jogging along sidewalks or sweating away in the gym and whilst at the same time we forget to devote any time at all to our mental health. Our brains seem to have become the forgotten organs of our bodies and yet they play a crucial role in our every action, emotion and activity. Perhaps it is time we gave them a little more attention and care.

Mindfulness has its roots deeply imbedded in meditation techniques practiced by nearly all the major religions. Where mindfulness practitioners differ from the more religious acolytes is that they have come at the subject from a secular and scientific point of view and do not require one belief system or another to be adhered to in order to participate. That is not to suggest that you need to separate any religious belief you may have from that of mindfulness. In the same way as penicillin, though discovered in Scotland, is of universal benefit to society, so mindfulness with its roots in meditation should be available to all.

It is probably the Buddhists that we most associate with the practice of meditation though the Hindus were using similar techniques over a thousand years before they even started. The Christian Bible is also dotted with exhortations to meditate. Some Buddhists have been known to complain that participation in mindfulness techniques is an abuse of their beliefs. A small minority feels that mindfulness practitioners are taking on only a small part of what Buddhists believe in, in a sort of cherry picking operation. Some Christians also developed a wariness of meditation when it became associated with beatniks and hippies when they first started venturing to India in search of enlightenment in the sixties.

In 1979 Professor Jon Kabat-Zinn founded the Mindfulness Based Stress Reduction (MBSR) program at the University of Massachusetts. His credentials along with his many scientific demonstrations suddenly threw MBSR back into the main stream. No longer shrouded in mystic or religious paraphernalia mindfulness study suddenly became acceptable and rafts of studies were carried out that leant more and more credence to the benefits of its practices.

126

There are now more than thirty universities throughout the world that have departments dedicated to MBSR or programs on it. These include Harvard, MIT, Cambridge and Oxford where a Masters degree in mindfulness is offered. By 2004 MBSR had become so acceptable that NICE, the British National Institute for Health and Clinical Excellence approved it in the management of depression and it thus became available on the National Health Service for the first time.

Despite the benefits of MBSR being recognized within both the scientific and medical communities, its adoption by the wider public has remained more limited. Many wealthy individuals including sports professionals and high profile business executives have come to see its use as an integral tool to their physical performance but those with lesser means have been slower to adopt the techniques. Only now are some people beginning to call for MBSR to be taught as part of the school curriculum and preliminary tests on its benefits are showing the results to be overwhelmingly positive.

One voice calling for the adoption of mindfulness in schools is Anne Marie Rossi, founder of the non-profit organization, Be Mindful. In conjunction with the University Of Colorado she conducted a research study on fourth grade students in a deprived inner city school. The results were staggering. Teachers reported a 250 percent improvement in emotional regulation, 600 percent higher pro-social performance and 550 percent improvement in academic achievement.

The advantages offered by MBSR are certainly not restricted to children of school going age. In a 2014 report compiled from forty seven clinical studies on three thousand individuals there was a 'measurable improvement of up to twenty percent in symptoms of anxiety and depression.' Incidents of recurrence were also reduced by between forty and fifty percent, which completes very favorably with prescribed anti-depressants.

Chapter 2

What is Mindful Based Stress Reduction?

There are numerous definitions for MBSR. Probably the best one to look at is that offered by Jon Kabat-Zinn who has done so much to bring MBSR into the mainstream arena of medical science. He defines it as 'The awareness that arises through paying attention, on purpose, in the present moment, non-judgmentally.'

It has been proven that stress plays a major role in ill health, particularly in the specific area of mental health. In the high pressure world that we live in today with its constant demands that we both achieve and acquire more, we find ourselves exposed to ever increasing levels of stress. This pressure we find ourselves living under is by no means restricted to high flying executives or people in high risk professions such as combat soldiers. From an early age even our children are victims of the pressure they live under and this is seen now as it has never been seen before except in the case of those children growing up in war stricken environments.

To be blunt stress can be a killer. It is one of the main factors influencing insomnia and there are powerful links between stress and chest pain, heart disease, heart attack and strokes. Stress and depression frequently go hand in hand and according to the World Health Organization depression is one of the leading causes of disability worldwide. In the US alone stress related illness costs in excess of 300 billion dollars per annum.

As if the stress level among adults were not concerning enough, there is evidence pouring in that there have been huge increases in the stress levels shown among our young people. In the US it is now the top health concern for teens between the 9th and 12th grades. Mental Health America estimates that a whopping twenty percent of teens are now clinically depressed. In the United Kingdom, the phone line Hopeline that is run by an anti-suicide charity has received a 400 percent increase in calls from young people since 2013.

MBSR aims to address the problems of stress by building on age old techniques of meditation. It is not an attempt to change thinking but instead offers its user increased ability to manage their thought processes in a deliberate and positive manner. We all run a mental thought line through our minds in which, in most instances, we act out the role of the major character. This need not be problematic but all too often we tend to focus on negative and worried thoughts that lead to increased levels of stress. MBSR teaches its adherents to control their thoughts and to act rather than react. The objective is to become aware of negative thought processes and the ways in which our minds work. Instead of allowing our thoughts to be divided between past or future worries we train it to let go of that negative thinking and focus instead on the present moment. This both reduce unnecessary self generated stress whilst at the same time allowing us to be more present and focused on the moment in hand.

The technique involves some self discipline and some patience, especially when first starting out. The rewards, however, can be great. Not only do we focus more fully on the present moment thus appreciating and participating with undivided attention, we also gradually develop the ability to control and alter our thought patterns to suit required situations. MBSR is seeing an ever increasing field within which it can play a role. It is being used as a tool in pain management, as a resource toward better inter-personal relationships and as a means to increase focus for people such as sports professionals. It is no wonder that there is now an increasing call for these methods to be taught in schools and other education facilities.

For too long now we have accepted the myth that although we can alter our physical abilities through a combination of diet and exercise, our mindsets are something that we inherit and which we have no control over. Again and again science has disproved this argument but science is not always good at getting its message across. The time has come when MBSR should cease to be the property of just academics and a small, well educated or wealthy elite. The tools toward more deliberate and self managed thinking are within the reach of all of us and over the next few chapters we shall start to look at how to use those tools and what benefits may be accrued from their use.

Chapter 3

The Basic Tools Toward MBSR

Our brains are very versatile organs. They control our every thought and action and yet we seem to have overlooked our emotions and thoughts during the many other health fads that we have subjected our bodies to. Only in fairly recent times, with an upsurge in depression, stress and mental health problems have we finally started to look in more depth at ways to bolster our thought processes in the realization that they are the building blocks of most of our other health issues. Of course the mystics and religious acolytes may have been doing this for centuries but their voices were somehow drowned out in the fast paced modern world of technology and industrialization. The previous chapters touched on how disastrous forgetting our emotional and mental health has been for our society. Now it is time to look forward again and see what steps we might take to put ourselves into a healthier mental state.

The premise of mindfulness is that we are able to master our own thought processes and to direct them to a way of functioning that is both positive and healthy. Unfortunately our minds have been allowed to run amok for years, much like children without discipline.

In order to retrain our thought processes we are bound to come up against resistance in the early stages but I urge you to stick with the process.

Most practitioners of mindfulness suggest starting with a simple breathing technique. It is not the only method but it is one that has been repeatedly tried and tested and is a good place to start. Whilst there is no right or wrong way to practicing mindfulness it is good to kick off with a method that has a proven track record. At a later stage you will almost definitely develop methods that are more specific to your own requirements and you can continue to explore these as you gain confidence and experience.

For now try to find a few minutes each day when you can be alone and undisturbed by outside influences and distractions. Sit down comfortably but in an upright position and close your eyes and relax. Once you have done that begin to breathe in deeply. Take deep but comfortable breaths into your belly via the nose and then out through the mouth. As you do so, focus on the physical aspect of each breath and the sensation of the air entering through the nose, down into the lungs and then leaving your body. At the same time, try to let go of any other thoughts.

Your mind will almost immediately throw up some objection or concern for you to worry about. Note that thought, then let go of it and refocus on your breathing. Do not judge the thought or even try to fight it, simply return your mind to the very physical process of breathing in and out. More mature practitioners of this form of meditation like to start the day with at least twenty minutes of mindfulness. You need not need to be that ambitious in the beginning. Instead aim for ten minutes and even if you only manage less than that do not beat yourself up about it. One of the principal pillars of mindfulness is that you have to learn to be gentle on yourself.

The mind will continue to present you with a long list of things to worry about, chores that should be done and other reasons that you should abandon the discipline exercises to which you are now subjecting it. I am warning you of this in advance because it is an inevitable part of the process but one that will gradually begin to diminish as you gain experience and your mind becomes more accustomed to being steered rather than simply being allowed to just react.

It normally takes about two weeks of this daily mindfulness exercise for the new practitioner to begin to see results. Roughly the same amount of time it would take for you to start feeling comfortable if you had just started on a gentle jogging program after a period without exercise. Try to perform the exercise each day and to add a few minutes to the routine each time but go easy on yourself and if you miss a session or two just start again as soon as you can.

After about two weeks you will begin to experience a rather strange phenomenon; you will begin to find yourself looking forward to your session and feeling a little uncomfortable if you are not able to squeeze it somewhere into your day. Gaining control over your thoughts will also start to become far easier. At this stage you may want to start considering some adjustments to the program to suite your own lifestyle and routine. We will look at some of the many adjustments you can make a little later but for the moment let us try to understand what is taking place and how it can benefit us. Just like a fitness regime, your mindfulness program needs to provide advantages to your lifestyle overall and not just during that few minutes of the day when you are meditating.

As you gain in experience you will find that you are able to translate the benefits of mindfulness into problems that you face during the day. When you face moments of worry or stress you will be far better able to examine them briefly then push them to one side. This is not an attempt to bury them, but rather a way to experience the present moment fully. If you mind is half on a problem and half on a job at hand, a state we lived in almost constantly before developing mindfulness skills, you will be less able to perform the job at hand. Instead you will constantly be torn between worrying about some past or future event whilst only performing in the present at a reduced level.

Studies of successful people from all walks of life have revealed that the single largest factor in determining their success was their ability to focus. Worry and concerns can affect our concentration and eventually our mental health but mindfulness is one of the most

135

powerful tools at our disposal for alleviating worry whilst at the same time helping us to focus on whatever is the more immediate task. One of the main aims of mindfulness is to train to better manage and deal with worry, which can have such far reaching negative effects on so many aspects of our lives.

The breath technique is just one method of practicing mindfulness and we shall be looking at others in the next chapter. It is important, however, that you understand that it is not the actual breathing that is important here. We focus on each breath because the human mind cannot simply function as a void. It needs something to point toward otherwise it hops from one thought to another with no managed direction. By focusing solely on our breathing, an action we are taking anyway, we narrow the arena the mind can operate in and thus leave no room for other thoughts, especially anxious ones. At the same time we confine our thoughts to the present rather than the past or future. As we will see we can focus on any number of other actions or objects and achieve the same result, providing we focus on one thing to the exclusion of all others. In reducing the amount of information the mind is having to process to just a simple, non stressful, present moment thought we allow room for deep inner peace. Even when done for short periods of time this provides a sort of reservoir of calm and tranquility to carry you through the day. At the same time as you become more accustomed to getting into this calm state it becomes easier and you are able to achieve it more quickly when confronted with stress.

Chapter 4

Further Methods for Specific Situations

We have looked at one of the simplest and most common of the mindfulness methods. It is easy to practice because breathing is a natural activity and all we need is a place of quiet and a few minutes to escape into our meditative state. In this chapter we will look at some alternative methods. Sometimes we may not be easily able to find that few minutes of quiet escape and it may be helpful to have some different methods we can more easily shoe horn into our busy lives. We may also need to practice mindful awareness for some specific goal, such as losing weight or overcoming anxiety. There are no hard and fast rules but all of the specific methods and alternatives below will be easier if you have already accustomed your thought processes to the discipline of the breath method for a couple of weeks.

Alternative point of focus

For most people the breath method is an easy place to kick off. For some, however, focusing on just the feeling of air going in and out of their bodies may not be enough to reduce their minds to a single line of thought. For others the breath method may become stale or boring.

One alternative is to take a natural object such as a flower and examine it closely. I do not mean just look at it in the way you normally would. Instead examine it with deep and utter intensity that demands all your concentration and allows no other thought to creep into your mind. Notice how each petal is aligned and how they connect with the stem. Study the veins as they become visible in the petal and the detail of each tiny part right at the heart of the bloom. If any other thought, concern or emotion starts to permeate your examination of the object then acknowledge it and put it to one side. Remember, the idea is not to smother that invading thought, simply to put it aside to be dealt with at a more appropriate time.

Another method is to hold your left hand in front of you with the palm facing toward you. Now run your right forefinger slowly up the side of your hand and up to the tip of the little finger. Proceed down the inside of the little finger to the flesh where it joins the ring finger. Continue running the right forefinger up each of the fingers of the left hand and then the thumb. As your forefinger travels, monitor it closely and notice the physical sensation. Above all else you are attempting to focus on the action you are performing to the exclusion of all other thoughts.

I hope that with these simple examples I have demonstrated that you see there is no end to the number of easy to perform activities that you can practice that will occupy all of your concentration. The activity itself is not what is important here. What is crucially important is that you are training your thought processes to focus on the present and not allowing them the freedom to jump toward other thoughts that you are not controlling such as fear or anxiety.

Anxiety relief

Anxiety is something that affects everyone at some stage though for some people it can be far worse than for others. Mindfulness is a wonderful and effective way to reduce stress but as anxiousness can attack at any time it may well not be appropriate to suddenly sit down, close your eyes and follow the air as it travels through your body. Try deepening each breath you take and counting each breath as you take it. When you reach ten then simply start again until the anxiety subsides. Focus on the breathing and push whatever thought it is that is causing you to become anxious to one side. If you have already been doing a daily mindfulness routine you will find that you are able to regain your equilibrium much more quickly as your thoughts will already be accustomed to being disciplined.

Diet and Eating disorders

Eating disorders are widespread in our society. They are not restricted to just the most critical ones such as bulimia and anorexia but also include any eating habit that causes us to gain too much weight. So much of what we eat is fast food that we grab on the run or ready meals that we gulp down in front of television without even really tasting. By focusing deliberately, not only on the overall meal, but also on each forkful that we place in our mouths, we may find that we are better able to control not only what we eat but also how much we eat.

Dieticians are very fond of telling us that we eat too fast and they are right. By treating every meal as a mindfulness exercise we not only slow down our rate of consumption but also the quantity. As you learn to appreciate each mouthful you may even be tempted to start to pay closer attention to the quality of the food you consume. Focus on each piece you place in your mouth right from the moment you begin to cut it with the knife and fork. Once you have a forkful in your mouth focus on the action of chewing, the taste and the texture before you swallow. Don't allow other distractions such as the television but instead treat this as the most important thing you are doing at the particular moment you do it. It needs to take on an almost religious element; an act of worship.

Sports performance

One group that has taken to mindfulness in a big way is sporting professionals. Many big name pros now include a mindfulness trainer on their teams in much the same way as they would a coach or physiotherapist. In addition to the ten or twenty minutes a day of mindful exercises, they also focus on using the techniques to reduce pre-game stress and to improve performance through eliminating conflicting thoughts and emotions that might otherwise have distracted them from their game. In much the same way some classical musicians are finding that these techniques can enhance their powers of concentration.

Pain management

The idea that pain and the mind are closely linked is nothing new. What has been shown recently through MRI scanning is that the pain receptors in the brain can be considerably reduced through meditation techniques such as mindfulness. Chronic pain is widespread and in the US it actually affects more people than diabetes, heart disease and cancer combined. The usual treatment requires powerful drugs which bring with them a vast array of both side effects and other problems and which can be prohibitively costly. Many people including health care professionals are beginning to turn to mindfulness as either an alternative, or in addition, to the more traditional pharmaceutical treatments. What we are learning is that whilst mindfulness meditation might not cure pain it is effective at enabling the victim to manage it more effectively.

Rather than simply trying to mask or bury the symptoms, mindfulness teaches victims of pain to focus on the area or areas concerned and break up each pain into smaller more manageable component parts. From there they might take their thoughts to other areas of the body where there is no pain or the pain is less acute. The management of pain becomes quite specialized and for more serious conditions it is advisable to engage the services of a professional in this field who is able to operate in conjunction to your doctor.

Working with children

Previously in this book I mentioned that early experiments with training kids to meditate was having such a profound effect that there is now a growing call for mindfulness classes to be incorporated into the school curriculum. We are seeing growing numbers of children suffering from attention deficit disorders, behavioral and relationship problems and difficulty with discipline. Many of these problems can benefit from mindfulness training and in some cases be eliminated altogether.

We need to have more patience when teaching kids these techniques but they are pliable and don't arrive with the same degree of skepticism that some adults need to get over when they first start. Because so much of what children deal with is new to them it is possible to use a wider range of methods to get their minds to focus on just one thing given the proper guidance. This area of mindfulness could fill a book on its own but just imagine how much better your child's life could be if he learnt to focus and overcome anxiety from a very early age.

Chapter 5

What Mindfulness Does

Neuroscientist Richie Davidson from the Center for Healthy Minds at the University of Wisconsin-Madison has this to say about mindfulness "We can intentionally shape the direction of plasticity changes in our brain. By focusing on wholesome thoughts, for example, and directing our intentions in those ways, we can potentially influence the plasticity of our brains and shape them in ways that can be beneficial. That leads us to the inevitable conclusion that qualities like warm heartedness and well being should best be regarded as skills."

That is an amazing statement because it shows that we can manage and alter our brains just like we can alter our muscles through the correct training programs. Tests have shown that people who meditate regularly increase grey matter and cortex thickness. Activity in the brain that would normally focus purely on ourselves has been shown to reduce after just one month of sustained meditation. In other words we become less self orientated.

Harvard University has conducted numerous tests on the effects of this program and some of the results have astonished even skeptical neuroscientists. MRI scans showing that there are changes in the brain's reaction to pain, emotional regulation and complex thinking abound. Much of this is still being studied but there is converging evidence that we have an extremely powerful tool for improving both physical and mental well being in the practice of this technique.

Clearly we have touched only the tip of the ice-burg during the course of this book. The basic concept that we should be aiming toward a twenty minute per day period dedicated to our overall well being through mindfulness has, I hope, been clearly demonstrated along with some simple methods for getting started. This age old practice, once exclusive to various religions, has now been brought into the secular environment and backed up by widespread and highly credible scientific study.

Mindfulness offers an easy way to improve the health of our brains, develop our decision making capabilities and handle stress more efficiently. All of these activities have a knock on effect in both our physical health and our ability to relate to others that can only be a good thing. Through secular study and science we now have evidence for a powerful program that we can incorporate into our religious practices should we wish to do so.

I have endeavored to show that mindfulness meditation is not something that is not exclusively the domain of any one group, be it rich or religious, and that it is something that can be easily learned at home. There is no right or wrong way as long as you bear in mind the basic principal of managing your thought processes and being kind to yourself.

Conclusion

Though there are many different ways to practice mindfulness they need not be complicated or onerous. The main idea is to reach a point where you can let go of all the multitude of thoughts and distractions that bombard your brain during the waking hours and just focus on one thing. You need to be kind to yourself and recognize that this process will get easier as you persevere. When I say easier, I mean that eventually you will be able to put yourself in a calm frame of mind even when confronted with stressful occurrences.

By learning to live in the moment you are far better able to appreciate the many good things around you and place a clearer perspective on those that are bad. I trust that this book will set you on a path of discovery that will eventually lead you to discover the deep inner peace within that we all crave so much. Meditation techniques that have been practiced for millennia have attracted many adherents but for those outside of these religious beliefs there was always a degree of skepticism. Now that science has examined these methods and found them to have great validity we are all able to enjoy their benefits and bring with us our belief systems, or not, according to what we feel is appropriate.

Because the methods are simple and because the brain is so versatile, we are able to employ these methods in more and more areas as we build upon our experience and confidence. There is likely to be a period of both skepticism and difficulty when we first start out but that is something we need to overcome with any new endeavor of worth.

If you discipline yourself to stick with these methods for a few weeks the difference will be noticeable enough that I believe you will not want to give up. After that you will find that the techniques take on an element of pleasure and the discipline part then falls away. The methods you have learned here will have set you up but you will soon find that you are weaving in your own methods, times and techniques. This is good because we are all different and each of us needs to find ways that make these practices valid in our own lives. It is also important because we need to grasp that mindfulness is not about rigid rules that confine the way we act. Instead it offers us the opportunity to carve out our own route to happiness and inner peace.

Thank you again for purchasing this book!

I hope this book was able to help you to get started on a path to a new way of living.

The next step is to devote a few minutes each day to quiet mindful meditation.

Manufactured by Amazon.ca
Bolton, ON

16958578R00085